WHEN GOD SURPRISES

Richard Bewes was born and brought up as the son of missionary parents in Kenya. He was educated at Marlborough, and later at Emmanuel College and Ridley Hall, Cambridge.

He is Rector of All Souls, Langham Place, having worked as a parish clergyman in the vicinity of London since 1959. He has also become much involved with the Keswick Convention, the Greenbelt arts festival, and Eurofest in Brussels. He is UK Chairman of African Evangelistic Enterprise, dealing with relief and missionary work throughout Africa.

Richard Bewes has written several books and has become a well-known media personality. He is married with three children.

Richard Bewes

WHEN GOD SURPRISES

Profiles of the Unexpected

First published 1986
Triangle
SPCK
Holy Trinity Church
Marylebone Road
London NW1 4DU

British Library Cataloguing in Publication Data

Bewes, Richard
    When God surprises: profiles of the unexpected.
    1. Lent ——Meditations
    I. Title
    242'.34   BV85

    ISBN 0-281-04201-2

Typeset, printed and bound in Great Britain by
Hazell Watson & Viney Limited
Member of the BPCC Group
Aylesbury, Bucks

INTRODUCTION

We have been taken by surprise all along the line, from the very start of God's great revelation. Of course we are clever enough to find out plenty of things for ourselves. When some beefy porridge-eating serf of an ancient Briton paddled off in the world's first coracle, he needed no divine voice to tell him how to put the craft together. No doubt the traditional 'We've always done it this way' brigade were horrified. But, before long, everyone was paddling about in mass-produced Model-T coracles, with perfect equanimity. At some point the wheel was invented. Today it is the space shuttle. Fair enough. We can reach the moon without needing God to tell us how to get there.

What we cannot do for ourselves, however, is to find the way to God and to explore his mind and his ways. For that we depend completely upon his communication to us – and this has happened. Moreover, there are surprises at every corner. In this book I have tried to examine some of the paradoxes and unexpected turns the Christian revelation takes.

You can read this book privately, or it can serve as the basis for a church or group study course or a Lent series. At intervals, I have interspersed group Bible studies, six in all, and I hope these prove to be useful.

Should you be reading this at the Christian season of Lent, then feel free to take one of the short chapters every day; the book will take you through to Easter.

Let us now engage in an exploration of the surprises of God.

RICHARD BEWES

All Souls Church,
Langham Place,
London

CONTENTS

PROLOGUE

Right About Face

Now I have found that Christianity is one of the most misunderstood subjects today. For myself, I do not think that people can be blamed for not understanding Christianity. If you had come to me a few years ago and predicted that I would become a Christian, I would have been frightened to death.

Vijay Menon *Found by God*

1 The faith principle

*Now faith is being sure of what we hope for and certain of what
we do not see.*

Hebrews 11.1 NIV

The great key words of the Christian faith can sometimes become
worn like those old Victorian pennies we sometimes find in the
bottom of a desk. They have passed through so many hands that
the inscriptions have rubbed away, the images worn thin. The New
Testament Hebrew Christians needed not so much a definition of
faith as a reminder, a *re-minting* of a great concept, now defaced.
We need this too. What is faith? Blind credulity? Wishful thinking?
A leap in the dark? The biblical revelation has some surprising
up-turns for us.

Believing is seeing

Faith has a way of annihilating the barriers that prevent us from
seeing and comprehending the spiritual realm. The opposite of
faith is sight. If I could *see* Concorde coming in to Terminal Three
from Tokyo, I would hardly need to check on the arrival time at
the information desk. As it is, the screen at the desk is enough.
It tells me all I need to know for my rendezvous with the arriving
passenger. I walk to the appropriate gate in confident faith.

'We walk by faith, not by sight,' affirms the apostle Paul
(2 Cor. 5.7). The inference is that the data given to us is sufficient.
It was enough for Abraham, the prototype of all believers, who set
out for an unknown promised land. It was enough for Moses, who,
in obeying the call to lead the people of Israel, 'endured as seeing
him who is invisible' (Heb. 11.27). It is enough that God has acted,
intervened, spoken, visited. Christians comprise the blessed company of those who have not seen, yet have believed.

Believing is knowing

Faith is not credulity. It is never blind faith. The information is
strong enough for men and women to make a reasoned response,
and to feel secure in that response. William McConnell, deputy

2

governor of the Maze Prison in Northern Ireland, wrote in a letter shortly before his assassination in 1984 that, in the event of his death, no one should feel alarmed about his eternal security: 'I committed my life, talents, work and action to Almighty God in sure and certain knowledge that, however slight my hold on him may have been . . . his promises are sure and his hold on me complete.'

Believing is relating

In the last analysis it is faith in a *person*. 'I know whom I have believed', declared the apostle (2 Tim. 1.12). Faith is not presumption. To say that you have great faith in your doctor says nothing about you – but it says a great deal about the doctor! Faith is not some unusual commodity that a few lucky individuals happen to possess; it is the informed response that anyone can make to the one who, in Christ, has spoken historically to the needs of our whole race. Faith culminates in a friendship.

PRAYER

God, heavenly Father, I look to you for the renovation of faith and devotion this day. May my vision of Jesus Christ your Son be enlarged, so that – though I have not seen him, I may love him and believe in him, and so rejoice with unutterable and exalted joy.   Amen.

2 When guest played host

*'Every man serves the good wine first; and when men have drunk
freely, then the poor wine; but you have kept the good wine until
now.'*

John 2.10

It was Bishop Dehqani-Tafti of Iran, himself a convert from Islam,
who wrote: 'It was the fact of the Incarnation which made me fall
in love with Christianity' (*Design of my World*). Of course this is the
greatest paradox of all, God becoming man. How can we ever
understand it? To quote Simon Jenkins:

like your landlord becoming your lodger
like your managing director up before you for an interview
like Beethoven queuing up for a ticket to his own concert
like a headmaster getting the cane
like a good architect living in a slum built by a rival
like Picasso painting by numbers
God lived among us

A whisper of the truth was getting through when Jesus attended
the wedding feast at Cana. It is a strange thought, to have God
attending your wedding. What did the young couple think about
it in later years? Did they become followers of Christ? However
much or little of the truth of the Incarnation sank in, it made a
considerable difference when the divine guest took the role of host.

Christ takes hold of the ordinary

A wedding reception; there could be no more common occurrence.
Thus at the outset of our Lord's ministry the theme was established
– and it is the theme of the Incarnation. God has fully entered into
our human situation, with its problems big and small, its macro-
issues and its little crises. God is concerned with the ordinary.

The ordinary becomes better

'You have kept the good wine until now', was the enthusiastic
accolade given to the gratified bridegroom. And this is the

4

testimony of Christian experience: that life with Christ is more colourful, richer, broader – and with a greater added value – than anything emerging from alternative quarters in the world's history. Literature, music, democracy, work and recreation – wherever Christ's influence has been exerted, there has been an elevation.

The best is yet to come

'This, the first of his signs, Jesus did at Cana in Galilee, and manifested his glory; and his disciples believed in him' (v. 11). It was wonderful enough, but it was only the beginning, this turning of the water into wine. Life after life, continent after continent awaited the rejuvenating touch of God in Christ, with its pledge of forgiveness, integration and life that is eternal.

'You don't believe all that about water into wine, do you?'

'Well, I wasn't there of course,' replied the believer, 'but I do know that Christ turns beer into furniture.'

'What?'

'O yes; I used to have a real problem with alcohol – so much so that I had to sell most of our furniture. It's completely through the power of Christ that I've been set free; and it's really because of him that we've got all our furniture back!'

THOUGHT

What practical difference is the Incarnation going to make to my life this day?

3   A bonus for the have's?

'Take heed then how you hear; for to him who has will more be given, and from him who has not, even what he thinks he has will be taken away.'
Luke 8.18

Here is another paradox. How revolutionary were the words of Christ to his hearers! Give to the Have's, and rob the Have-not's; is this really the teaching of the compassionate Jesus?

We must remember to listen to this teaching of Jesus through Jewish ears. The Jews of all people constituted the *Have's* in spiritual terms. They had Abraham as their father, the laws of Moses as their inheritance, the leadership of the prophets as their bulwark. And yet, what had they to show for all this? There is a contrast here.

The doers and the hearers

'Take heed then how you hear.' The never-to-be-forgotten parable of the sower and the seed had just been given – with its challenging theme of the different kinds of ground – or hearts. What are we going to do with the knowledge and advantages we have been given? On that issue rests our growth, our destiny.

A map in the British Museum demonstrates that as early as 1540 the Portuguese believed in the existence of Australia. Had anyone acted or capitalized upon this knowledge, the likelihood is that today's Australians would all be singing *Waltzing Matilda* in Portuguese. But it was not to be. There is all the difference of a continent between doing and hearing.

The have's and the have-not's

It is a matter of practice rather than of theory. To quote Mao Tse Tung: 'If we have a correct theory, but merely prate about it, pigeon-hole it, and do not put it into practice, then that theory, however good, is of no significance.'

'Having', then, is more than passive possession. The parable of the talents tells us that. The man with one talent – and who did nothing with it – is like Israel's typical leader of our Lord's day. Because he failed to use his privileges and opportunities, posterity finally showed him to be a have-not – and he lost everything. In the teaching of Jesus, having is using.

The users and the losers

Everybody has an opportunity, a talent, an unrepeatable life-span in which to know God and serve him. 'Only one life is allotted us,' warned Alexander Solzhenitsyn, 'one small, short life!' (*The Gulag Archipelago*).

The lesson is that if we are content to stand still in our living and our learning, we shall find that we are slipping backwards. The Church, the Bible, the Sacraments, the Fellowship, the present opportunity – you either use it or you lose it.

PRAYER

'Lord, give me eyes to see, and grace to seize, every opportunity for Thee.'

Bishop Taylor Smith's daily prayer

4 When the seeing become blind

'For judgement I came into this world, that those who do not see may see, and that those who see may become blind.'
  John 9.39

I was a little boy in Africa when Cunningham's comet appeared in the night sky. Naturally I had to be shown this strange phenomenon, as my parents have never ceased to be fascinated by comets. I was hauled out of bed, and carried out wrapped in a blanket to see the spectacle.

'I can see it!' exclaimed my younger brother Michael. I peered up anxiously, nervous of failure. 'Where? Where?'

'Look, *there*!' And a parental finger pointed out the direction for me.

'I can see it!' chirped Michael again. I stared my hardest.

'*I can see it*,' I said woodenly. And with that we were carried back to bed. But I'm afraid I never did see that comet.

It is an emotive subject, sight. We find it hard to say that we do not see what others can all too clearly observe. Particularly was this so in the case of the man born blind. It was, if you like, an acted out parable, full of irony and paradox.

There is involuntary blindness

He had been blind from birth, and no one was to blame, said Jesus. Of course, we are always looking for reasons, when faced by the phenomenon of suffering, and these are not easy to pinpoint. Suffering sometimes occurs simply because we are part of the fallen creation. At times it is a direct result of sinful actions, but that was not true in this case. At times, we can understand it in the light of our call to identify with Christ in his sufferings. We can also see it as an occasion for spiritual growth (Acts 14.22). But in this case, it had been permitted for a revelation of 'the works of God', as a demonstration and revelation of divine power. Not only was there healing, but in addition a recognition of Jesus as Messiah. It was a great day for the man born blind!

8

There is wilful blindness

The fact that the healing took place on the Jewish Sabbath complicated matters. The controversy boiled up – to a point at which the newly-seeing believer found himself excommunicated from the synagogue (John 9.22). The fact was, that the religious leadership refused to accept the revelation that had been given them in Jesus. Of all people they were the best placed to receive such a revelation; centuries of religious tradition and preparation lay behind them. But at the point of opportunity they closed their eyes. This led to a strange and paradoxical sequel.

There is retributive blindness

It was a turn-around, and full of irony. The blind nonentity emerged from the story, seeing and believing. The privileged leadership came out of the encounter with the scales yet more firmly over their eyes. It is a law of the spiritual life. Pharaoh in Egypt hardened his heart against Moses; the upshot was that finally it was God who hardened the heart of the obstinate dictator (Exod. 14.4).

It is a hard lesson to accept. But without the theme of judgement we make a mockery of such words as *forgiveness*, *reward* or *merit*. God has a way of underlining our choices and actions. There is always opportunity for a change of course, but if, openly and knowingly, people choose to believe a pack of lies, God will give them their fill of lies. The judgement is – that in claiming to be wise, they become fools (Rom. 1.22). To the very end they will be saying 'I can see it!' when they can't.

PART ONE

When Dying is Rising

As we embark upon discipleship we surrender ourselves to Christ in union with his death – we give over our lives to death. Thus it begins; the cross is not the terrible end to an otherwise God-fearing and happy life, but it meets us at the beginning of our communion with Christ.

Dietrich Bonhoeffer   *The Cost of Discipleship*

5 Faith's pinnacle

By faith Abraham, when he was tested, offered up Isaac . . . He considered that God was able to raise men even from the dead; hence, figuratively speaking, he did receive him back.

Hebrews 11.17,19

It was in Amsterdam some years ago that I met an Indian *guru*. Or, to be more precise, an *ex-guru*. He was now a most effective Christian evangelist. But the turning point for him was full of pain, uncertainty – and death. His book, appropriately enough, is entitled *Death of a Guru*. In it he testifies: 'The moment I asked Christ to be my Lord and Saviour I would lose everything: my Brahmin caste, my status as a young Yogi, the blessing of the Hindu gods, the goodwill of my family. I would automatically be an outcaste from the Hindu community, lower than the lowest. *And* what if Jesus couldn't really forgive my sins and change my life after all? Suppose I wouldn't really know God through him? How could I risk so much when I wasn't sure?'

But risk it he did. It was in a real sense a death and resurrection. If we have been in the Christian family any length of time, we will be familiar with this radical theme. We can trace it back a very long way. Abraham's sacrifice of Isaac was the supreme test, venerated by the Jews. Here was the long-promised heir; how much joy he had given to his aged parents! And now, it seemed, he was to be offered up . . .

There is familiarity here

Abraham was only too familiar with the human sacrifices of the Canaanite religion; sacrifices that were made out of the fear of stern, unloving deities. Was Abraham's God just like all the others? No, in later times God – the only God – is identified as 'the God of Abraham, Isaac and Jacob'. Nevertheless, the idea of sacrifice was not foreign to Abraham.

There is superiority here

As Abraham set out with Isaac for the sacrifice, he told the others to wait, promising them, 'We will come back to you' (Gen. 22.5 NIV). Was he lying? Certainly not. God had promised that through Isaac would come the promised descendants. In that case, reasoned the patriarch, God would, if necessary, raise the boy from death. It was an extreme example of tenacious faith; indeed Abraham was to be known as the father of all believers. Death and resurrection belonged together in this outstanding example of trust.

There is prophecy here

The whole idea of sacrifice in the Old Testament was to prepare the way for Christ. It was all an education in the holiness of God, the ugliness of sin and the costliness of salvation. Dying and rising – all was to be fulfilled in the sacrifice of the Lamb who was slain from the foundation of the world.

MEDITATION

Were the whole realm of nature mine,
That were an offering far too small;
Love so amazing, so divine,
Demands my soul, my life, my all!

Isaac Watts

13

6 The prayer of desperation

Then Jonah prayed to the Lord his God from the belly of the fish.
  Jonah 2.1

I sometimes wonder whether the Bible commentaries have always got it right, when it comes to interpreting the experience of Jonah. One of them included a section on *When he prayed*, following this by *Where he prayed*, with the observation 'No place is amiss for prayer'. It even quoted from the New Testament, 'I would that men prayed everywhere'! Another commentary featured 360 pages of worthy, if protracted, observations. I found myself counting the words in rapt fascination; one sentence alone contained 147 words.

Most of the commentators seem to think that Jonah's prayer from inside the great fish (it was a *mega ketos*, rather than a whale as such) was a quite excellent model of a prayer – and in a way I suppose it was. After all, whose prayer is going to score ten out of ten when they have been eaten by a fish? The prayer in fact was all about himself. Again, that's fair perhaps. We would hardly be praying for the latest American peace initiative in similar circumstances. The personal pronoun predominates in Jonah chapter 2. *I* or *me* occur twenty-four times in all.

While we cannot see in these words an ideal pattern for prayer generally, we can, however, see here the prayer of a desperate person about to die. In this sense there is a great deal to learn.

The place of adversity

So often it is adversity that makes us throw ourselves upon God. Jonah's prayer is full of God-consciousness: 'Thou didst cast me into the deep . . . all thy waves and thy billows passed over me.' Before the sailors had thrown the prophet overboard he had been sleeping. All that was changed. He was praying now. Adversity so often jolts us into a new God-consciousness.

The place of memory

They say your life flashes before you when you are drowning. It certainly was happening to God's man. Instinctively he remembers . . . *the Temple* (vs. 4,7). Do we not know this experience? That when the storms break over our heads the old songs and hymns . . . little pieces of liturgy . . . portions of Scripture come filtering into our consciousness. It is not heavy theology that we need in the face of affliction – it is a *reminder*; that and little else just then.

The place of honesty

Read Jonah chapter 2 at leisure. There is not, of course, a word about the mission in Nineveh that awaited the prophet. There is no real word of repentance. There is an awareness of God, of life, and of the Psalms (Ps. 18. 4–6 find an echo in Jonah's prayer). God has his foot in the door of Jonah's will, and that is about it.

The prayer of desperation can take different forms. It may even be expressed only in a comfortable silence of understanding. After all something radical is taking place. We are in the middle of a dying and a rising again.

7 The great leveller

'Go and wash . . . and you shall be clean.'
2 Kings 5.10

An Englishman was preparing for one of the great experiences of his life. As he left his comfortable cabin for the last time, he weighed up carefully between the various possessions that could be taken with him. Something had to be left behind. Dressing carefully in thick clothes, Major Arthur Peuchen left behind some 300,000 dollars in bonds and preferred stock, selecting instead three oranges to take with him into the freezing night. An hour or so later the *Titanic* had gone to the bottom of the Atlantic.

It is the life or death experience that brings us all on to a single level. The Bible teaches us this, as nothing else does. 'What shall it profit a man if he gains the whole world and loses his own soul?' But long before Jesus spoke these words, a mighty general, Syrian by nationality, prodigious in his achievements, had to taste the humiliation of being a nobody like everybody else. Naaman had already secured for himself a place in the galaxy of five-star generals – then he contracted leprosy. Seemingly he was a dead man. There was no special treatment for generals. Indeed, was there a treatment for anybody? Well, there was. But it had to be done in God's way.

God's remedy is always humbling

It started with an Israeli girl, captured on one of the earlier Syrian raids. Remembering the work of the prophet Elisha, her recommendation filtered through from the servants' quarters in the Naaman household. So far so good. But it meant a trip to Israel, a visit to the prophet – and then the prescription . . . a dip in the muddy, pint-sized Jordan! Naaman was not pleased.

> 'Behold, I thought that he would surely come out to me, and stand, and call on the name of the Lord his God, and wave his hand over the place, and cure the leper. Are not Abana and Pharpar, the rivers of Damascus, better than all the waters of Israel?' 2 Kings 5.11,12

16

How human! But Elisha wasn't even coming out; he was somewhere inside having his breakfast. It is surprising for some to learn that God's way is the humbling way – for everyone. Go and wash!

God's remedy is always simple

It has to be, in the end. How unfair if only the great ones, the clever, the sophisticated or the rich could have access to the Presence. The way through has to be uncluttered enough for the simplest to understand. Go and wash!

God's remedy is always free

'So he went down and dipped himself seven times in the Jordan, according to the word of the man of God; and his flesh was restored . . .' (2 Kings 5.14). And payment? There was none. There never is. To go into the water, to die and to rise again, to find cleansing . . . and purity . . . and new life at the hands of God costs a man or woman, a boy or girl precisely nothing – beyond, *Go and wash*!

THOUGHT

The next time you partake in the Holy Communion, forget the attire, the little give-away tags of rank or attainment. You are there, shoulder to shoulder, in one category only in the great family of God.

8 The man who never died

By faith Enoch was taken up so that he should not see death; and he was not found, because God had taken him.
Hebrews 11.5

It's nice, isn't it? After all, would you have chosen Enoch for the great Hall of Fame in Hebrews chapter 11, among all those heroes and heroines of faith? What exactly *were* his achievements? What dent did he finally leave upon his world of Genesis chapter 5? In what way was the world different, because of Enoch's life? The answers to those questions have to be couched in the negative – except for one significant fact. He walked with God.

Enoch features in a long list of names. These lists are in the Bible partly to highlight the odd ones and twos about whom something stands out. They shine against the background of the rest, like a piece of glass reflecting light from inside a coal bunker. Enoch is the unknown warrior who unexpectedly finds himself venerated in the national shrine of remembrance. Enoch is like the unseeded player who gets into the semifinals at Wimbledon or Flushing Meadow. Only one sentence of his was ever recorded for posterity, and it got into the Bible at Jude verses 14–15. But apart from that – no great speeches, no startling deeds. But we must notice this; *he was a man who was missed when he was gone.*

One day Methuselah, his son, probably said to the others in the family: 'What's happened to Dad? I can't find him.' The news went round the village . . . *Enoch's missing.*

'Nobody could find him' reads the Good News Version of Hebrews 11.5. The implication is that there was a search party! Perhaps they would not have bothered too much about some of those others in the list of Genesis 5. And some of the truly evil characters of the Bible nobody would have concerned themselves about: Manasseh, Ahab, Nebuchadnezzar.

It is a strange thing that there are certain individuals who, although they never *did* very much, nevertheless leave a yawning hole when their departure from the scene is recorded. And so Enoch is included in God's great Hall of Fame. He was a reminder to others of what it means to walk with God. And by his uncanny translation into the life beyond, he left people with a reminder of that greater dimension that must colour all of our living.

Enoch was one of only two men in the Scriptures who never died – the other being the mighty, fiery Elijah. Presumably Elijah is in the great Hebrews 11 chapter? He is not. He only gets included under the blanket title 'the prophets'.

Anyone can walk with God. You may live in obscurity, you may never hit the headlines, you may never achieve a quarter of the things you set out to do, and you may remain a nonentity all your days – but it is the godly people of character, of fellowship and faith, who will be missed when they are gone. One day Enoch simply failed to turn up for lunch. He was missed. A search party went out, but 'nobody could find him'. He was walking with God.

PRAYER

There are people in our lives, Lord, who remind us of yourself. When they are with us we want them to stay. They are oblivious of this effect they have upon us. Teach us to value this power of unconscious goodness in a person's life, and to value it before it is taken away.   Amen.

9 The man who died twice

'Lord, if you had been here, my brother would not have died.'
    John 11.32

These words tell us that even before the miracle of the raising of Lazarus, Christ's authority had a high place in Mary's estimation. She knew. She had sat at his feet often enough when Jesus had come to the home in Bethany. Even now, it was a comfort to see him. But Lazarus had died four days ago and the Master had come . . . well, a little too late.

Authority is stamped all over this passage in John chapter 11. It was a very human, compelling piece of drama. Christ himself was deeply moved in all of the proceedings. But throughout, he demonstrated an authority and power that continues to disturb the waters of mankind's prejudices.

The power to remove

'Take away the stone,' ordered Jesus (v. 39). A rustle went through the group of onlookers. What was he going to do? Perhaps utter a farewell prayer by the tomb? A beautiful idea – but why tamper with the tomb? No one knew. The great gravestone seemed to represent all the crushing weight of superstition and dread that had gathered around the forbidding subject of death over the centuries.

The stone seemed perhaps to be a symbol, as Christ ordered its removal. More than a mere stone was about to be interfered with. *The removal of ignorance* was part of the issue. No one had ever come back from the grave. No one had authority in that sphere. From this day on it would be different. *The removal of despair* was part of this cameo. Jesus wept, it is true (v. 35), but not with hopelessness. In his action he sanctioned for ever the place of tears when bereavement strikes. But, Christ's was not the weeping of blind despair. *The removal of prejudice* was involved in his action too. No one – not even rank unbelievers – would ever be able to think about death in quite the same way, after the ministry of Jesus.

20

The power to reverse

'Lazarus, come out!' (v. 43). There is that authority again. Another command. Nothing like this had ever happened before. There had been hints in earlier times, as in the case of Elijah and the young lad in 1 Kings 17, but this was unique. The funeral had taken place four days earlier. That was irreversible. What kind of authority had been our Lord's when he stilled the storm? That was amazing enough. Now they were speechless. The world they had always known was swaying crazily around their ears.

The power to release

'Unbind him, and let him go' (v. 44). Go? Go where? Why, back to his home in Bethany. It would be lunch-time in a few minutes. And tomorrow would see Lazarus hobnobbing with his neighbours once more, off to the supermarket to do the week's shopping, filling in his tax returns . . .

It is a strange thought. By the action of Christ, Lazarus had been brought back into the *old life* again, with its relationships, its routine, its aches and pains and problems. And one day, he was going to die again; going through the whole process once more!

What is this saying to us? Christ has the power to release people from the winding sheet of death. But this event, electrifying as it was, could be no more than an illustration, a curtain-raiser to the big event that still lay ahead. For Lazarus, resurrection meant a coming *back* into the old life. He was going to die twice. For us, resurrection means a going *on* – to greater powers, greater glory and a pain-free life in a resurrection body that will never see corruption.

The onlookers that day thought that they had seen the ultimate. They had not. Easter, the event that stands at the parting of the dispensations, still lay ahead.

10   Identified with Christ

We were buried therefore with him by baptism into death, so that as Christ was raised from the dead by the glory of the Father, we too might walk in newness of life.

Romans 6.4

Working as we do at the centre of a great city, we have had the privilege of baptizing individuals from many widely differing backgrounds – Buddhist, Muslim, Hindu, and Christian. It is always an excitement to me to stand with the individual, or company of those newly baptized, at the close of the ceremony, and to introduce them to the worshipping family of the church. Smiling faces focus in from the main body of the church and from the galleries; brown faces, white faces, black faces. Applause breaks out. How happy we are! We are the family of Christ, identifying with him in the centre of London.

It is not that baptism – as an external act – makes us one with Christ. This was one of the mistakes of the Jews of Paul's time. They had persuaded themselves into believing that because they had received the Old Testament ordinance of initiation (in circumcision), they were therefore secure in the covenant and plan of God. The apostle had to correct them: 'For he is not a real Jew who is one outwardly, nor is true circumcision something external and physical. He is a Jew who is one inwardly, and real circumcision is a matter of the heart, spiritual and not literal' (Rom. 2.28,29).

Circumcision, and its New Testament counterpart, baptism, are the outward and visible signs of an inward reality – identification with Christ by the free grace of God, entered upon through faith. Received rightly in this way, baptism means such a lot!

It is a goodbye to the old life

At baptism we enter a new era of our lives. We are turning our backs upon the old life that has crowded Christ out. We are declaring war upon selfishness, lust and pride. We are letting it be known, in this public way, that we are identifying with Christ's death. On the Cross he accepted the responsibility for our sins. He died. Now that we are identified with him it can be said that *we*

22

'died'; *we* have borne sin's penalty – but in him, and through him, our Representative at the hill of Golgotha. The past is over and we are saying goodbye to it. We have died with Christ.

It is an embracing of the new life

Christ was raised from death historically as the divine demonstration that his sacrificial death for all of humanity was complete, a perfect atoning for the sins of the world. But those who identify with him are raised too. The marvel of the resurrection body awaits us in the glorious future. But even now, the life of the resurrection is a reality. It has begun. We have been raised to newness of life!

A CHALLENGE

The inward reality must correspond to the outward sacrament. How are we living up to our baptism promises? Some people were baptized in infancy. Those promises made on our behalf – have we made them our own yet? Baptism is not complete until faith is present.

11 The tribulation and the kingdom

Through many tribulations we must enter the kingdom of God.
Acts 14.22

Do we teach this to inexperienced members of our churches? We need to. We are living in a success-orientated culture which cannot really come to terms with adversity or sickness. Indeed, it has gone a stage further in some circles, where much play is made of 'prosperity teaching' – the doctrine that a believer in God can expect full health, a topped-up bank balance, extra help with the mortgage and prospects of promotion. Of course, if this were an essential part of the Christian good news we could expect a flock of *customers* rather than disciples in the Church.

This is not the path that Christ promised we should tread. 'In the world,' he said, 'you will have persecution.' He spoke of carrying one's cross, of self-sacrifice and opposition. We are not surprised, then, to find Paul and Barnabas emphasizing that it is through many tribulations that we must enter the kingdom of God.

Tribulation

The word for tribulation in the Greek is *thlipsis*, which refers to a confining, squeezing pressure. It is used of the travail pains of an expectant mother (John 16.21). *Tribulation* comes from a Latin word that conveys the idea of grinding, threshing and stamping. If we choose the way of Christ, the way will be made uncomfortable on both sides of us.

Must . . .

The way of progress through pressure is a certain prospect, we learn from Acts 14.22. This is because of the kind of world we live in; it is a world that has rejected the rule of Christ. We must not be surprised in the face of opposition (2 Tim. 3.12). We must also recognize that strangely God has chosen such a pathway for our spiritual benefit (1 Pet. 1.6).

Enter in

Most of us see trouble as a dead end. The Scriptures regard it as a way out into progress and strength. It is the way by which we enter the kingdom!

The kingdom of God

God's kingdom is not territory as such. The term describes the rule that God exercises. If we want to know his rule in our lives, then tribulation is the way in. It says so, repeatedly in his revelation. 'If we endure we shall also reign with him' (2 Tim. 2.12). We read in the book of Revelation of 'I, John, your brother, who share with you in Jesus the tribulation and the kingdom . . .' (Rev. 1.9).

Suffering and adversity present us with a strange paradox. We do not court suffering – but when it comes it may, in the economy of God, be turned to positive account. It is not an option for the Christian way. It is the Christian way.

GROUP QUESTIONS

Are you in a student group, a house fellowship or on a church course? Having read the earlier chapters of this book as background, members of the group may like to engage in some joint discussion. A study of Romans 5.1–11 would make a good basis for a start. The following questions may stimulate the discussion:

1 'Justified' (v. 1), or God's free *acceptance* of us through the work of Christ, is the basis on which the Christian life is built up. Try and identify from these two opening verses some of the great spiritual benefits that stem from justification. Can you put these into your own words?
2 Then in verse 3 comes the paradox of rejoicing in suffering. Try to establish from vs. 3–5 why this should be so. Can group members think of individuals who exhibit this phemomenon?
3 In vs. 6–8, what is unique about Christ's suffering on behalf of others?
4 Keep thinking upon the death of Jesus Christ. What do we mean by the phrase 'Christ died for us' (v. 8)? What is our right response when this truth sinks home?
5 Looking at verse 9, what difference does the Cross make to the way in which we regard the judgement of God?
6 Look at verse 10. Dying and rising both feature in this passage. What does this now mean in the experience of the Christian?
7 Suffering and rejoicing both occur in the passage. What is it in the end that makes Christianity worthwhile?

PART TWO

When Slavery is Freedom

To be a slave, however painful, humiliating and
distressing the situation, is also a form of security,
while to become a free person is a state of utter
insecurity . . . It is only when our freedom is rooted
in God that we become secure in a new way, and in a
very different one.

Anthony Bloom   *Living Prayer*

12   Models of behaviour

Bid slaves to be submissive to their masters and to give satisfaction in every respect . . . so that in everything they may adorn the doctrine of God our Saviour.

Titus 2.9,10

I remember meeting a young woman in Keswick, where the famous Christian convention takes place each July, bringing thousands to the little lakeside town. She had been on the staff of a hotel which housed some of the speakers during the 'Keswick Week'.

'You know,' she said, 'down in the town I hear attenders at the convention saying how much they like Mr. So-and-so's speaking, or the Rev. Bloggs' address. But I find myself thinking in a different way about the speakers. I judge these preachers not by their speeches but by their bedrooms!'

It is our lifestyle that must be the telling factor in the end. By our fruits we are to be known – from the highest to the lowest. The apostle Paul was not averse to selecting the lowest for his examples of how to live out the revolutionary faith of Christ. Writing to his fellow-worker Titus in the island of Crete, he cast about among the different categories of person in his emphasis upon an adequate Christian ethic. He then turned to the slaves; they were to be submissive, honest and faithful.

Does that sound a little tame? Would you and I have looked for something a little more radical – a summons to organize themselves, to defy the authority of their masters, to plan a revolt, a ban on overtime, a demonstration, a movement of self-liberation? Of course, there are occasions when a strike is justly called for. But here in lazy, gluttonous Crete the call was for something a little more revolutionary than a mere Spartacus or Marx might have planned. The way of Christ is more radical still. The New Testament Christian radicals didn't simply *fight* the oppressive slave system. In the freedom of the family of Christ, they chose to ignore the class distinctions completely and behave as though they did not exist. In their own church fellowship there was neither Greek nor Gentile, neither slave nor free. *These demarcations were irrelevant.*

The call, then, to the Cretan slaves was, 'Out-perform your

masters! Make Christianity attractive to them and to everybody else. *You* be the working model of Christian citizenship and set the example to society – and demonstrate by your life that the Christian does not pilfer, does not need to pilfer.' The Christian slave had the freedom of the City of God, and that was where his strength and superiority lay.

In this way the slaves of Crete were to 'adorn' the doctrine of God; as William Tyndale translated the Greek, they were to 'do worshippe to the doctrine'. From the highest to the lowest, the behaviour of the Christian has the power to enhance the revelation of God in Christ. Our speech, our deeds, our attitudes are to be like the picture frame that makes the perfect setting for a beautiful canvas. The slaves of Crete? Some frame! Yes, but this is the paradox of radical Christianity. It enables the observer to look at the values and standards of a Christian slave and say, 'What a beautiful doctrine!' It is the most revolutionary approach of all.

PRAYER

Teach us, O God, to see where true freedom lies. Free us from the shackles of convention, class struggle and materialism, and lead us in the way of Christ who makes us fellow-citizens with the saints and members of the household of God.   Amen.

13   Babel's folly

'Come let us build ourselves a city, and a tower with its top in the heavens, and let us make a name for ourselves, lest we be scattered abroad upon the face of the whole earth.'
   Genesis 11.4

I was about to address a meeting in the university sportsmen's club at Oxford, when the news came through of the chaotic rioting in the Heysel football stadium in Brussels. Thirty-eight people died before a ball had been touched in that European cup final. It was a dreadful night for sport, and the commentators were almost lost for words in their confusion and anxiety. How could human beings behave as though they were animals?

The difficulty is that the media have been bludgeoning us for years with the lie that there is really no significant difference between people and animals. It is by a strange irony that we are so surprised when members of society begin actually to live as though there were no moral or spiritual dimensions to life.

We are the victims of our own propaganda, the products of the godless world-views that have been promulgated in the world since the very beginning. The folly of Babel is a classic; it is a story of secular humanism, of man off the leash, of man without God, self-made, thrusting, conceited man. It starts as a search for liberation, expansion; it ends ironically with a reduction of man's stature. Babel has to do with the age-long quest that we all struggle with: the quest for identity.

The quest for identity

'Let us make a name for ourselves.' Biblically there is nothing wrong with research, discovery and creativity. Sport, the arts, architecture and science all flourish when a God-consciousness lies behind them. But take out the God aspect, and the result is confusion, ugliness and perversion. The search for identity ends in absurdity.

The search for community

'Let us make a name for ourselves lest we be scattered . . .' Babel was a collective effort, an attempt at unity. It achieved precisely the opposite result from the one desired; the project was never completed and the workers became scattered and separated.

The search for security

'This is only the beginning of what they will do' (Gen. 11.6). The note of divine foreboding marks a Creator's and Father's concern, not a rival's, writes F. D. Kidner in his commentary on Genesis. The tower of Babel is the forerunner of Babylon which, biblically, stands for worldly, pretentious self-elevation and protectionist insularity.

Whenever God is left out of our plans, fragmentation results. Communication becomes difficult, negotiations founder, agreement recedes from our view. Need it be so difficult? The Lord's Prayer contains a mere 56 words; the Ten Commandments, 297. The American Declaration of Independence contains 300 words. But the Common Market regulations on the import of caramel contain 26,911 words! Somewhere, somehow, there are surely some lessons to be learnt from the man-made slavery of Babel.

14 Which authority is it to be?

'And the Lord commanded us to do all these statutes, to fear the Lord our God, for our good always, that he might preserve us alive, as at this day.'
  Deuteronomy 6.24

'If we are not governed by God,' said William Penn, 'then we will be governed by tyrants.' That was back in 1681. It takes men and women a long time to learn the lesson – that we have to live under authority of one kind or another. The freedom cry of the 'sixties was bound to lead to a reaction eventually. It was in the 'eighties that a new authoritarianism set in. On the religious front it took the form of pyramid structures in certain cases – groups and sects dominated by one charismatic leader at the top, with members discipled rigidly at every level.

In the more extreme groups, on both sides of the Atlantic, a member would find it impossible to move house, marry or change banks without the action being sanctioned by another figure, or alternatively by 'the group'. In some associations members are required to sign over their house, their possessions and money to the central pool. They own nothing; they belong to the group and, in that sense, they have become slaves.

To some it is an attractive way in which to live. After all, there is a certain security in slavery. True, you are not your own, but someone else is doing the worrying on your behalf. You have no real decisions to make – somebody else is seeing to your provisions, your housing and your activities. Someone else is telling you what you must believe; the thinking can be left safely to others who have the authority over you.

For the biblical Christian the whole edifice falls to pieces with the simple realization, *I am a disciple of one Man only*. I shall always value the God-given authority of my Christian leaders, but I am not their disciple; I am not their slave.

To be in a state of such freedom would be utter insecurity were it not for the authority of God to which the believer gladly submits. This is the true slavery of the Bible, the acceptance of a leader whom to serve is, strangely, perfect freedom.

It is the authority of the Designer

He knows our frame, our capacity, our moods and habits. To submit to his rule is to find fulfilment and the true outlet for our energies. He sets us free to be ourselves; to be creative like himself.

It is the authority of the Father

His laws and statutes are given us 'for our good always'. Our limits are defined by him. It is a benevolent rule, with protection and life built into it. Understanding and trust lie at the heart of this relationship.

It is the authority of a Liberator

The freedom given by God is different from the freedom we were pursuing in the 'sixties. True freedom is, to use Solzhenitsyn's definition, 'self-restraint in the interests of others'. It is not freedom from responsibilities; it is freedom for service. It is not freedom from the fight; it is freedom *for* the fight. If we have become slaves to God, and to his Son Jesus Christ, then we have become 'free indeed' (John 8.36).

PRAYER

Deliver us, Creator God, from the bondage that makes us slaves to the conventions and personalities of others. By your liberating Word, transfer us to that other authority, the reign of your kingdom of light and love. For Christ's sake.　Amen.

15 Where is the attraction?

*'So therefore, whoever of you does not renounce all that he has
cannot be my disciple.'*
Luke 14.33

Where is the attraction in Christian discipleship? During his
ministry in Galilee the crowds swirled around Jesus. Perhaps some
of them thought that they were on a victory march; they wanted to
be present when the Messiah claimed his throne. He was the
Messiah, of course, but his was a topsy-turvy kind of messiahship,
with desolation and death at the end of the trail. Repeatedly Jesus
turned on the crowd, explaining sternly what discipleship would
mean. All who mean to follow the Christ will be exposed to various
exacting tests.

The love test

Love for Christ takes precedence over the highest form of love
known in our world – that of human love within the family. We are
encountering Old Testament Semitic language in the 'hate' vocabu-
lary of Luke 14.26. For example, we learn from Genesis 29.31 that
Leah was 'hated' while her sister Rachel was 'loved' by Jacob. It
was the terminology of *selection*. Similarly in Romans 9.13 – 'Jacob
I loved, but Esau I hated.' Thus, to 'hate' one's relations by
comparison to our relationship with Christ is to say that, at heart,
Christianity is a way of life with *one* great loyalty, one main driving
force, one supreme love at the centre; a love and a loyalty that
overrides all others. All other loves, while they will be enhanced
and lifted by this first love, will come second to it. It is the love
test.

The death test

'Whoever does not bear his own cross and come after me, cannot
be my disciple' (Luke 14.27). Carrying your cross means putting
your own interests last – to the very point of death. Unless initiates
to the Christian faith hear and understand this teaching, we are in
danger of producing little Peter Pan Christians who never grow up

at all; they only came for the balloon ride. Let them have a tiff with another church member, fall out with one of the church leaders – and they are off. They have never seen Christ at all.

The finishing test

Jesus told two parables here; one about a man who failed to count the cost of his building project, the other about a monarch who omitted to think through the costly implications of engaging in battle. History has produced many Don Quixotes; it is all too possible that the would-be disciple of Jesus Christ will be consigned to history's book of heroic failures – simply for lack of sitting down and thinking through the implications of obeying the call of Christ.

Where is the magic of discipleship, in view of these stringent tests? The answer lies in the magnetic pull exerted by the man of Galilee himself. We have only to brush against him to feel the tug of his example, of his selfless love and goodness. *I will follow this man*, we find ourselves saying; *I will love him above all else, and continue with him to the end of the road*. And then, to our amazement, as we reach the end of the trail, a vista opens up ahead and we discover that we had lost nothing at all in our adherence to the Galilean. It has all been worthwhile, for the sake of his eternal friendship.

16   The transforming touch

Then the angel of the Lord reached out the tip of the staff that was in his hand, and touched the meat and the unleavened cakes; and there sprang up fire from the rock and consumed the flesh and the unleavened cake.

Judges 6.21

It only take a single generation for everyone to forget. So it was, in those twelfth and eleventh centuries BC, as Israel struggled to survive amid the alien Canaanite culture. Purity was eroding, and syncretism was the order of the day. People would say, 'You know, these Baal-worshippers are very decent people; their beliefs are quite like ours – I'm sure we can learn a lot from them.'

Then there was the problem of the Bedouin marauders, the Midianites, with their new secret Exocet – the camel. The overall scene was one of humiliation. It is here that we find Gideon (*Hewer* or *Smiter*) moodily threshing wheat in secret, in Judges chapter 6.

It only takes a touch from God, however, and the scene can change. The call to lead Israel out of the morass comes to the inexperienced farmer through an angelic visitation. He spreads out a meal for his visitor – and at a touch the food is consumed by fire. It only takes a touch, and we can see its effect, first in alleviating the drudgery.

Alleviating the drudgery

Up till then Gideon's only apparent achievements had been displayed in his exploits with a flail. But now the words rang in his ears: 'The Lord is with you, you mighty man of valour.' Forget about the golden past, the great days of Moses and Joshua. A new era is beginning – and it starts with you. The oppression is ending.

Animating the ordinary

Gideon's faith was not strong; he needed a sign, and in the grace of God he got one – first through the incandescent touch of the angel upon the prepared meal. There could be nothing more ordinary than a plate of lamb chops! The extraordinary dealing of

God is that he involves himself in the ordinary, taking it up and investing it with significance. It was this feature of God's action that turned Gideon the hewer into Gideon the worshipper (vs. 22–24).

Elevating the nobody

Gideon really was a nonentity, 'the least in my family' (v. 15). But this experience of encounter was to transform him into a leader with a new name and identity – *Jerubaal* ('Let Baal contend for himself').

A hundred years ago Hudson Taylor, the pioneer missionary in China, declared: 'God chose me because I was weak enough. God does not do his great works by large committees. He trains somebody to be quiet enough and little enough, and then he uses him.'

It only took a touch, and a flame was lit in Gideon's own life. The end of this episode had the trumpet heralding the struggle for liberation that lay ahead – with its battle cry, 'The sword of the Lord and of Gideon!'

MEDITATION

A servant with this clause
Makes drudgery divine;
Who sweeps a room, as for thy laws,
Makes that and the action fine.

George Herbert

17   Liberating truth

'You will know the truth, and the truth will make you free.'
  John 8.32

Truth can surface in the strangest places. Was it not the Soviet leader, Mr Andropov, who used to say, 'There is an old Russian saying . . .' and then proceed to quote Scripture! Truth can be found, like the frail edelweiss flower that clings to a crevice in the Swiss Alps, surviving in the most inhospitable environments. 'Truth is solitary and silent,' declared Malcolm Muggeridge once in Switzerland, 'It doesn't have to be propped up by noise.'

Truth as a passion

'What is truth?' asked Pilate as Jesus Christ stood before him. He may only have been playing with words; even so his question expresses the insatiable curiosity we feel as we survey our universe and try to prise out its secrets. Isaac Newton, the grandfather of modern science, made his discoveries, he said, 'by keeping a subject constantly before me until the first dawnings open little by little into the full light'.

Truth as a power

'The truth will make you free', said Jesus. In the last analysis it has never been the military machines or the political figures who have dictated the course of history; we owe that supremely to people's *ideas*. Truth cannot be held down for long. It thrives on adversity. The freedom of understanding is the flower it produces.

Truth as a person

Christ's Jewish hearers resented his statement that the truth would set them free. They were descendants of Abraham, they protested, and had 'never been in bondage to any one' (John 8.33). In a sense they were right. They had suffered bondage in Egypt and Babylon, and now they were under Rome – and their Jewish spirit had never been broken. It was, however, an inner, moral slavery that Jesus was referring to. This was unpopular teaching, but more was to follow. 'So if the Son makes you free, you will be free indeed,' he went on (v. 36). The clue to understanding – and true liberation – lay in himself. It was not that he simply spoke the truth. He was – and is – the Truth.

Truth as a paradox

There is such a depth in the truth of God that we can never even get close to exhausting it. We must pity an individual or movement claiming a monopoly of the truth. None of us is going to have the truth neatly parcelled in a tight little system. The greatest people of understanding and learning are quick to declare with humility that they know nothing. We struggle with the issues of life; of guilt and forgiveness, of suffering and evil, of war and famine, death and eternity. Truth presents us with questions and paradoxes – and all we can say with our finite understanding is, 'At least I am a beginner. At least I can see, in God's revelation of himself in Jesus, where the *centre* lies.'

'The truth will make you free.' Once we get away from the centre in our exploration of the truth, we become *eccentric*; the whole thing becoming a muddle and a nonsense. Once we get the centre right, the whole thing will have a basic cohesion, even if there are gaps to be filled.

18   The breath of the Spirit

*For you did not receive the spirit of slavery to fall back into fear,
but you have received the spirit of sonship.*
   Romans 8.15

Let us round off this section of our study with a consideration of
attitudes. It is interesting to learn that India, with its million and
more temples to myriads of different gods, only has a few temples
dedicated to the supreme creator-God, Brahma. An ancient Hindu
hymn explains why:

> 'Men worship Siva, the destroyer
> Because they fear him;
> Vishnu the preserver,
> Because they need him.
> But who worships Brahma, the creator?
> His work is done.'

Jesus taught differently. 'For only a penny you can buy two
sparrows, yet not one sparrow falls to the ground without your
father's consent. As for you, even the hairs of your head have all
been counted' (Matt. 10.29, 30 GNB).

When we apply this to prayer, the contrast between the two
approaches is very marked. There is reverence and awe in our
approach to the Father, but not fear. Confidence has replaced the
abject slave-mentality. It is to Jesus supremely that we are indebted
for our concept of God as Father, in the intimate sense that the
New Testament expresses it.

The servant or the slave does not know what his master is doing,
said Jesus (John 15.15). How different is the situation when we are
in the family. When our children were little, we would let them
come bouncing into our bed in the early morning – bringing half
the toybox with them. They had access to us! So, in the realm of
prayer: 'When we cry, "Abba! Father!" it is the Spirit himself
bearing witness with our spirit that we are children of God,'
(Rom. 8. 15, 16). We began the chapter with a Hindu hymn; we
end it with a Christian one:

40

Freedom and life are ours
    for Christ has set us free!
never again submit to powers
    that lead to slavery:
Christ is the Lord who takes
    a man to be his own
and by his saving gospel makes
    a slave into a son.

Christopher Idle

GROUP QUESTIONS

1 Corinthians 7. 20–4 will make a useful study. The group may like to use the following questions to help the discussion:

1 When we read the First Letter to the Corinthians, it is a little like listening to one end of a telephone conversation. The apostle Paul is dealing with various issues confronting his readers. What main principle is he establishing in these five verses?

2 What lies behind this principle? How does it contrast with the Hindu view of passive resignation? Look at verse 21.

3 Look at the paradoxical language of verse 22. Can you put into your own words the mentalities which Paul is describing here?

4 'A slave of Christ'. What does this mean? Think of a nurse, a shop assistant, a bank clerk, a person who is between jobs. How is such a term applied to life and work?

5 In what way do people become 'slaves of men' today (v. 23)? How is this prevented? Where does the motivation lie?

6 What are the factors that should caution us to stay as we are in life and occupation? What factors ought to prompt us to change?

7 Can you define Christian freedom? Freedom from what? Freedom for what?

8 Can the group think of individuals and sections of society where there is little or no freedom, for whom our prayers are desired?

PART THREE

When Weakness is Strength

So if you are involved in some sort of failure in your everyday life, in a disappointing love affair or in an economic problem, it is a good opportunity for you. God takes advantage of your despair over failure. If through the power of Jesus you can rise up again, the success will compensate your failure billions of times over.

Toyohiko Kagawa   *The Religion of Jesus*

19   The flower pot men

But we have this treasure in earthen vessels, to show that the transcendent power belongs to God and not to us.

2 Corinthians 4.7

Although the revelation of God in Christ needs a frame, a setting, a stage, it is not dependent upon this for its effect. It is, in fact, impossible to manfacture or manipulate mystery; it simply cannot be done. The moment we try to guild the Gospel lily, we stand a very good chance of obscuring it.

There is no need for us to strive after effect, in expressing the mystery of God. Once a clergyman or meeting organizer says, 'It will be good for them to sing or do this, because it will have such and such an effect upon them', then a danger point is reached; there should never be a *them and us* mentality in worship, or Christian communication, in any case. Manipulation is out. Naturally we must work hard at the format through which our worship and teaching is expressed. Dangers encompass us on many fronts! We must beware lest Christians become reduced to a pietistic subculture of worshippers on the icy wastes of western Europe – either twittering to each other in unsingable Elizabethan chants or repeating, *ad nauseam*, Moonie-like little ditties as uncreative as they are puerile.

Even so, our most effective channels for expressing the Christian Evangel can at best be described only as 'earthen vessels'. And what is this message? It is the unique, incandescent announcement that the Creator has become involved in the affairs of this beautiful blue planet – coming historically in the person of his Son, to live and suffer among us and for us, accepting in the desolation of the cross the sorrows and sins of a race that had turned rebel; opening to us, in the event of the resurrection, a gateway to spiritual renovation and eternal life. This is the jewel that has shone into humanity's darkness like the famous Koh-i-Noor diamond. And where shall we display this blazing stone?

Perhaps we can find an old jam jar under the stairs. 'Earthen vessels' is Paul's word for it. 'Clay pots' is how one translation puts it. I think I can visualize it – it is something like a flower pot.

So, what shall we start with? When the Son of God comes to

earth, can we find a suitable site? That cowshed over there – we will begin with that. And that animals' eating trough – we can always clean it up a bit. That artisan home of a Jewish joiner – why not? That bunch from the Israeli fishing industry – they might make tolerable communicators.

It has been like this all the way along. The transcendent power is not found in that beautiful cathedral, wonderful as it is. That superb music by itself could never have changed anyone's life. That speaker with the gift of the gab – the truth is that apart from the message of reconciliation he has been given, he is little more than a piece of putty. We must give credit where credit is due. The power resides in God, and in God alone.

PRAYER

O God, take my abilities and make of them what you will. Let my life this day be a vehicle for your light, your love and your truth.   Amen.

20 An unusual instrument

*By faith Rahab the harlot did not perish with those who were
disobedient, because she had given friendly welcome to the spies.*
Hebrews 11.31

There is a little shop in dusty Muranga, Kenya, that I am familiar
with. I last saw it a few years ago. It is called Fido's Bar and was
situated just near a petrol station. It was there – slap in the middle
of tropical Africa – that our family once bought, of all things, a
Father Christmas outfit, fur trimmings, beard and all! How did it
ever get there? What did they think it was, out there in Fido's Bar?
At any rate, we acquired it from the Asian manager and used it
from then on, every Christmas.

When I see Rahab's name in the middle of God's honour roll,
there in the middle of Hebrews chapter 11, it is a healthy reminder
to me that the strangest instruments for good can be found in the
most unlikely of places. Talk about Fido's Bar! Who was this
Rahab?

An unexpected ally in hostile territory

We read about Rahab in Joshua chapter 2. It was the run-up to the
Battle of Jericho, and Rahab represented Joshua's tenuous toe-hold
in the city intended for capture. A wedge had to be driven into this
seemingly impregnable city, and Rahab turned out to be a divinely
provided thin end. Thus the success of the whole operation was to
turn upon the presence and co-operation of a prostitute.

An unexpected faith in a heathen environment

Yes, she had faith, of a sort. 'I know that the Lord has given you
the land . . . for the Lord your God is he who is God in heaven
above and on earth beneath' (Josh. 2.9–11). Is it a little hard to
accept that a prostitute had faith? The Jewish historian, Josephus,
tried to tone Rahab down to what he called 'a tavern-keeper'! But
no, we must accept that unlikely instruments find their use in the
economy of God.

An unexpected example in a cloud of witnesses

The Hebrews passage has already been instanced. And what of James 2.25? 'And in the same way was not also Rahab the harlot justified . . .?' There it is again – *harlot*. One commentator primly suggests: 'May we not venture to believe that the one who had become a believer in the God of Israel had also, ere this, repented of and forsaken the infamous life which her title imports?' Perhaps, perhaps – but isn't it interesting that the only person selected by God as a person of faith in Jericho was the town prostitute?

An unexpected ancestor in the royal line

Rahab turns up in yet another New Testament list of names – she features in the opening sentences of Matthew's Gospel, as an ancestor of King David (Matthew 1.5). We are looking, of course, at Christ's ancestral line. It is a turn-up for the books. Rahab the prostitute is the black cat that comes walking up the aisle during the singing of the 'Te Deum'. She is in the hall of fame to shock us out of our smug complacency. She is there to encourage us that the weakest, the most notorious in the city, can enter the service of the Lord God. It was Rahab who made the deal with the incoming Israelite spies, giving them refuge and facilitating the next move in the onward march of God's people. For that, she was to be remembered long after Jericho had been reduced to a pile of ruins. Or Fido's Bar, for that matter.

21 Where the power lies

Not by might, nor by power, but by my Spirit, says the Lord of hosts.

Zechariah 4.6

We know it really, but we have to be reminded of this great principle again and again. It is not as though we are without ample illustrations. In the late 1940s all Christian missionaries were removed from China, as communism took over. There were then about one million Christians on the mainland. Today there are at least fifty million – and this, without foreign aid or resources.

'By my Spirit' – this is the secret. God's words were given to the prophet Zechariah after a time of national humiliation and exile for the Jews. It was his calling to inspire the people of God in the task of re-building the nation's life – and the problems were immense. But the talisman of success had already been given to him.

Ideas are sharper than swords

'Not by might . . . but by my Spirit.' A few people, armed with a spiritual ideal, can accomplish so much more than an army stacked with equipment and weapons. Gideon and his valiant 300 are a classic example . . . David and Goliath – we are not short of biblical instances of this vital principle. It is not the military machines that have lastingly affected the history of the world, nor the exploits of the world's political figures, however able. It is the 'ideas people', who lie behind the twisting fluctuations, that have changed the world. Ideas are sharper than swords.

Spirit is superior to flesh.

'The more I think of it,' writes historian Arthur Bryant, 'the more I am convinced that everything of value in our history between the Dark Ages and our own time grew out of the Christian faith' (*The Lion and the Unicorn*). The danger moments for the Church are the periods of temporal and material ascendancy, the eras when monasteries grew fat and the faith was propagated through grandiose military campaigns. By contrast, we have the testimonies of those whose faith shone out of privation and suffering. 'Love', said Corrie ten Boom of Ravensbruck, 'is larger than the walls which shut it in.'

Good is stronger than evil

This is epitomized in the life of Jesus, who faced and overcame evil in a collision of opposing kingdoms. The Christian believer rejects the dualism that conceives of good and evil as co-existing on equal terms for ever. Evil is an intrusion into God's perfect universe. The demons of evil may seem to engulf humanity at any one moment in a whirlwind; but the lesson of Zechariah is still with us, and we must read our newspapers with the firm conviction that we are watching evil thrashing in the death throes of a kingdom that is on its way out.

FOR REFLECTION

'It is prayer, and prayer alone, that can make history.'

Jacques Ellul.

22 Identikit of a prophet

In the year that King Uzziah died I saw the Lord sitting upon a throne, high and lifted up; and his train filled the temple.
Isaiah 6.1

The prophet Isaiah and the evangelist John Wesley had much in common. Both had a protracted ministry of about fifty years; Isaiah in the eighth century BC, Wesley in the eighteenth century AD. Both had an encounter with God: Isaiah through his vision of the Lord in 740 BC in Jerusalem's temple; Wesley when his heart was 'strangely warmed' in a meeting at Aldersgate Street, London, on 24 May, 1738. And both had a profound impact upon the history of the world.

It is a vision, a conception of the Lord, that provides the foundation to every life that is to shine out for God. We can assemble the anatomy of God's call as we look at the famous sixth chapter of Isaiah.

I saw the Lord

It starts here. This is the antidote to all service for God that becomes stale and fossilized. It is the remedy for witness that becomes self-defeatingly egocentric or eccentric. Fifty years lay ahead for both Isaiah and John Wesley, but they never forgot their initial call. It is only those with a sense of calling who are still operational when the ground caves in, when the mobs are rioting, when the sky becomes opaque.

He touched my lips

'Woe is me!' exclaimed young Isaiah at the vision that confronted him. But his sense of unworthiness and impurity was met by the touch of God. It is *the touch of forgiveness* and the words 'your guilt is taken away', that made the call palatable. It was also *the touch of hope*. When God forgives, he also equips and fulfils for service.

I heard the Lord

'Whom shall I send?' Notice that nothing yet is said about the nature of the mission. Isaiah's ministry was to span the reigns of no less than four kings, in a period of national crisis and calamity; but he was not to know that when the call came. The world was to become Wesley's parish, but when the call came he had no inkling that he was to become the most travelled Englishman of the century. The call of God is given in terms that we can accept, one stage at a time.

Then I said, 'Here am I! Send me'

There comes a point when, in a bound of faith, a man or woman accepts the paradox that the God of all perfection and holiness has chosen to use an unworthy instrument. 'Without God,' said Augustine, 'we cannot. Without us, he will not.'

And he said, 'Go . . .'

Now the assignment becomes more definite and specific. People will hear but they will not understand. At points the mission will be characterized by utter failure. Isaiah would be persecuted; tradition has it that he was finally sawn in two. Wesley was to face the mobs of Wednesbury, St Ives and 'wicked Wigan'. But the stamp of these two men, called by God, is indelibly etched into history.

PRAYER

O Lord God, when thou givest to thy servants to endeavour any great matter, grant us also to know that it is not the beginning, but the continuing of the same unto the end, until it be thoroughly finished, which yieldeth the true glory; through him who for the finishing of thy work laid down his life, our Redeemer Jesus Christ. Amen.

Sir Francis Drake.

23   The foolishness of God

God chose what is foolish in the world to shame the wise, God chose what is weak in the world to shame the strong, God chose what is low and despised in the world . . . to bring to nothing things that are.

1 Corinthians 1.27, 28

Corinth was Sin City. It numbered in Paul's time about a quarter of a million people. Overlooked by the great temple of Aphrodite, it gloried unashamedly in strident immorality. Stage dramas of that time introduced Corinthians on to the stage invariably as staggering drunks. But, it was here that a church took root during the apostle Paul's two-year stay, representing a shining triumph of the cross.

The cross is an emblem of shame and weakness. And yet, it represents the essence of authentic Christianity. It is God's masterpiece. But on which side of the cross are you standing? That factor will largely determine which of the alternative views you take as you survey the crucifixion.

Foolishness or wisdom

To the Greeks, the cross and the crucifixion, were a laugh, a matter of foolishness – the Greek word is *moron*. The Greeks were looking for a system, a satisfying source of *sophia*, the kind of wisdom of which the Old Testament speaks; basically it is the art of being successful. But, as Paul declares, 'the world did not know God through wisdom' (1 Cor. 1.21). Certainly the inscription *To the Unknown God* on the altar in Athens (Acts 17.23) bore this out. No, it was through the foolishness of the cross that the true knowledge of God was made available. Today Plato is specialist reading for the esoteric few; John's Gospel is the biggest-selling piece of literature in the history of writing and publishing, finding its way around the world into the refugee camp and the leprosy settlement.

Weakness or strength

To the Jews the cross was a disgrace. It was inconceivable that the Anointed One of God could die in this way. This is the stumbling block of our Muslim friends too. What the Jews were interested in was power – the presence of signs and wonders. They could not, at that time, conceive that the cross would, in future generations, speak of forgiveness, of peace with God and power over death. How do we see the cross? It depends on where we are standing.

Offence and essence

Both Greeks and Jews, for different reasons, rejected the message of the cross. Wisdom was the great quest. Alternatively it was power. But what the follower of Christ found, claimed the apostle, was wisdom – and power – in one and the same Person! The cross held the key to it all. It lies at the centre. To preach Christ without the cross would be equivalent to writing a biography of Torvill and Dean without any reference to ice skating. It would be like making a television documentary on Neil Armstrong, with no mention of the moon. In Christ crucified lies both 'the power of God and the wisdom of God' (1 Cor. 1.24).

24 The dimension of the Spirit

'Truly, truly, I say to you, he who believes in me will also do the works that I do; and greater works than these will he do, because I go to the Father.'
John 14.12

Whatever did Christ mean by his statement about the 'greater works'? Has anyone in history ever out-performed our Lord in the field of miraculous accomplishment – either for quality or quantity? It only needs ten seconds' thought for us to realize that, if his prediction refers to miraculous deeds of a physical nature, then his words have fallen flat on their face.

After all, who in history, after the time of Christ, was recorded as stilling storms at a word, healing lepers at a touch, feeding five thousand people from virtually nothing, walking on water or raising someone from the dead after four days in the grave? No one has even come near the attainments of Jesus Christ.

Yet a great deal is laid upon this statement of his. Healers of all backgrounds and types base their work upon John 14.12. But we are not convinced that their efforts have exceeded those of the Great Physician. At times there is an element of uncertainty, even of frenzy, in their well-meaning efforts. They seem to require certain conditions for their activities – an arena, a stage, special lighting and music. And even then, when the cameras have stopped rolling and the crowds have gone home, we are not quite sure what really did happen. Jesus needed no stage-management, no formula, no practised routine or techniques. Certainly there was no doubt about the healings. They were instantaneous on virtually each occasion, and they were decisive.

But we need not be cynical about prayer for healing. It can and does happen – though without doubt the best place for it to be practised is in the local church – where everybody knows everybody, where there can be no cover-up, and where there is plenty of opportunity for follow-up and for monitoring progress.

But what of these words of Christ? The key to understanding them lies in the phrase 'because I go to the Father'. Supposing we had stopped the world after Christ's ascension, how could we say that it had been improved by his thirty-three years? A few blind people were now seeing; some lepers had been cleansed, and other burdens had been wonderfully lifted. A single generation would have removed even these individuals.

No. At the ascension a change begins. The new age of the Spirit was about to dawn as men and women in the Roman Empire, then Asia and far beyond, were to be introduced to the spiritual dimension available from Pentecost onwards. The miracle of the new birth by the Spirit was to be achieved on a global scale, life-changing in its effects, all-energizing in its power – and achieved quite independently of the physical presence of Christ. Jesus was limited in his earthly ministry to the few hundred who could be near him at any one moment. With Pentecost came an advance. 'It is to your advantage that I go away,' he told his disciples (John 16.7).

Here then were works, not of a superior physical kind, but works of a superior dimension altogether. The conversion of the three thousand at Pentecost was a greater event than the feeding of the five thousand by Lake Galilee. The newest Christian recruit, who can lead a friend or neighbour to faith in Christ and to the gift of his Spirit, does something that it was not possible for Christ to do in quite the same way. Pentecost brought in a new factor. Greater works? As we look at the growing Christian Church on all six continents, we can acknowledge that this is true.

25 The place of prayer

So Peter was kept in prison; but earnest prayer for him was made to God by the church.
  Acts 12.5

There is nothing like a crisis to set the church praying. Here we are in the early stages of the New Testament church. It could hardly be a tranquil process. Heads were getting cracked right and left; Stephen had died, James had been executed – now it was the turn of Peter, the Rock Man; clapped into a top security wing under heavy guard. Of course, we know the end of the story . . . the angelic visitation, the breaking of the prisoner's shackles, the opening of the gates one after another, until finally the prisoner reaches the open street; whereupon he makes straight for the church prayer gathering.

You see, prayer was central. It is God's appointed way by which we may co-operate with his divine purposes.

The covenant of prayer

There has to be an agreement about prayer among the church members: 'We are going to pray.' We pray, not because prayer is in any way an insurance policy against trouble. One of England's top footballers once declared, 'I turn to God when I need him.' But that is to treat prayer, and God, as a kind of wishing well. The power of prayer is indeed tremendous, but we do not pray primarily because we need God, but because we love him. Members of Christ's Church learn to take prayer out into every day; the events, big and little; the happinesses, the disasters; the dull 'in-between' periods. If we believe in God at all, we are going to pray. God's strategy is closely bound up with the life of prayer. Herod Agrippa thought he had disposed of the early church by incarcerating its leader, but prayer brought God into the arena.

The community of prayer

A tingling sense of expectancy characterizes the church that prays. Do you know this experience, even if only a little bit, in your own

Christian community? Coming together to pray is a test of our sincerity, our unity and our expectancy. We know that without God, nothing of any significance is achieved . . . so we pray. Our weakness becomes transformed by his strength. Church worship becomes irradiated with his presence, when there is prayer behind it. Evangelism becomes something purposeful and powerful as prayer takes off among church members. Things happen, and we expect them to happen.

The combustion of prayer

Things certainly happened that night for Peter. Freed from prison he headed for the place where he knew his friends would be found. They were 'amazed', the historian Luke tells us. A masterly understatement! Peter's arrival fairly lit up the prayer gathering that night! It is one of the features of prayer – even when apostles are involved – that we are invariably surprised when God takes action through our praying.

And what of the prison itself? On finding the locked jail empty, there was, we learn again from Luke, 'no small stir among the soldiers'. No small stir? There was bedlam – the detainee had apparently done some kind of Houdini trick on the lot of them, and no one would ever have known how it had been achieved, except for the careful chronicling of the episode by Luke. It was through prayer.

PRAYER

Eternal God, we give thanks that your strength is made perfect in our weakness. Teach us, in our churches, to live and breathe in the power of prayer. For your holy Name's sake.   Amen.

GROUP QUESTIONS

At the close of this section, an obvious passage for study would be 2 Corinthians 12.7–10. After prayer for guidance, let the group be encouraged to read the passage, and then to use the following questions to aid the discussion:

1 Both letters to the Corinthians are basically concerned with the theme of power through weakness. What essentially is Paul saying in verse 7? He had evidently had some deep experiences of God. In what way is 'elation' balanced by trials?
2 Paul's thorn in the flesh is not defined. Why do you think this is so?
3 How are we to view the trials that come our way (a) as far as Satan is concerned, (b) as far as God is concerned?
4 In verses 8 and 9, Paul's prayer is answered, but not granted. What is the group's experience in this aspect of prayer?
5 How do you see the principle of verse 9 working out in the experience of Christians generally? Where do we see this happening today?
6 Discuss Paul's theology of suffering, from verses 9 and 10. What areas of church life today need correction in this respect?
7 Why is it so difficult for the unbelieving world, and indeed for other faiths, to understand this concept of power through weakness?

PART FOUR

When Emptying is Filling

I am no longer my own, but thine. Put me to what thou wilt, rank me with whom thou wilt; put me to doing, put me to suffering; let me be employed for thee or laid aside for thee, exalted for thee or brought low for thee; let me be full, let me be empty; let me have all things, let me have nothing; I freely and heartily yield all things to thy pleasure and disposal.

From the Covenant Service   *Church of South India*

26   Two men, two ways

'You go one way, and I'll go the other.'
Genesis 13.9 GNB

Sir John Laing, whose family business achieved international fame for integrity and skill in the building industry, was involved in major construction works everywhere – motorways, factories, airfields. As a Christian, he was giving away a great deal of his fortune as early as the 1940s; and many were the new church buildings that owed their existence to the generosity of this man. Millions of pounds passed through his hands. When he finally died, in his ninety-ninth year, his net personal estate amounted to £371. He had practised the art of giving all his life. How many of us salute his memory!

Perhaps he had learnt some of it from Abraham. Abraham always sat lightly on his possessions, comparing favourably in this respect with his nephew Lot. The contrast was not between a saint and a rogue; it was more subtle than that. Genesis 13 presents us with a contrast between the advanced believer and the man who is content with an easy faith. The leader for God can do one of two things. He can look after his own interests if he wishes to – and God will let him do it. Alternatively he can look after the interests of the kingdom of God – and God will look after his interests. Abraham proved that the second way is the fulfilling way.

The test came when there was insufficient land to accommodate the entourage of both Abraham and Lot. The older man generously gave way: 'You go one way, and I'll go the other.' Lot immediately chose the security and comfort of the fertile Jordan valley, and the two men separated. But Abraham's was the way of trust and faith.

The flexibility of faith

Abraham was older than Lot; but it was Lot who was in the rut of middle-aged anxiety, quick to protect his own welfare. Flexibility, and the readiness to face change and perhaps discomfort, does not depend upon the age factor at all. There are senior saints in our churches, of seventy-five and eighty, who can cheerfully countenance adapting to a changing era; and there are striplings of twenty-five who are thrown by the smallest ripple. It is a growing and vibrant faith that makes all the difference. Abraham could adapt.

The generosity of faith

It was faith in God that gave Abraham his perspective on life. The greatest Christians of all often have a good deal of wealth flowing through their hands but they do not, in fact, care a button about money. They are here for others, and theirs is a world-view which embraces the world. Do you know of any such? Their generous self-giving keeps the world intact as a going concern. The others hardly care.

The prosperity of faith

All too often the grabbers end up with nothing, while the givers scoop the pool. So it was with Abraham and Lot. Such is the paradox of spiritual things. Lot elected to move his tent to the supposed security of the Jordan valley . . . and to the suburbs of the doomed city of Sodom (v. 12). Six chapters later sees him barely escaping with his life from the destruction that obliterated the site forever. He was the loser.

And Abraham? A gilt-edged promise became his on the day of his generous gesture: 'Lift up your eyes, and look from the place where you are, northward and southward and eastward and westward; for all the land which you see I will give to you and to your descendants for ever' (Gen. 13.14, 15). We can do one of two things when it comes to dealing with material security. Which is your way?

27   The paradox of the Spirit

Do not get drunk with wine, which will only ruin you; instead be filled with the Spirit.
Ephesians 5.18 GNB

The apostle Paul is writing here of two kinds of intoxication. It is possible to be controlled by alcohol; but the better way is to be controlled and dominated by the Spirit of Jesus Christ. How can we know if this better way is happening? What are the marks of a Spirit-filled Christian, or church? At first sight it looks quite surprising.

The Spirit-filled person is more aware of Christ than he is of the Spirit

So often the terms 'Christ' and 'the Spirit' seem interchangeable. In speaking of the coming of the Spirit, our Lord declared, 'I will not leave you desolate; *I* will come to you' (John 14.18). To receive Christ is to receive the Spirit – and it is the function of the Spirit to throw the spotlight upon the Son. 'He will give me glory,' said Jesus (John 16.14 GNB).

There is this strange anonymity about the Holy Spirit. I have sometimes been asked by Christian friends, 'Is yours a *Holy Spirit* Church?' What are the marks of such a church? The answer is easy to give from the Bible. A Holy Spirit church is *a church in which Jesus Christ is unmistakably at the centre*. A Spirit-filled Christian then is a Christian who is Christ-conscious through and through.

The Spirit-filled person is more concerned with 'emptying' than with 'filling'

The fullness of which the New Testament speaks resembles Lake Victoria rather than the Dead Sea. The Dead Sea has no outlet; its 'fullness' is one of death. Lake Victoria on the other hand, while it is receiving water constantly from the surrounding land, has an immense outlet at Jinja, and thence through North Africa to the Mediterranean.

Translate this into Christian terms, and we are speaking of

obeying, not waiting. Filling comes with activity, not passivity. We are now in the age of the Spirit. With service comes fulfilment and filling. Do you not feel better at the *end* of a piece of Christian service than you did at the beginning? This is surely related to the filling of the Spirit. It is a matter of *sharing, not hoarding.* No one can speak of the Spirit filling them if they are hugging their blessings to themselves.

The Spirit-filled person is more devoted to his fellow's interests than to his own

Our passage is set in the context of Christian relationships and mutual service. We can tell when the Spirit is active in a community; there is the tell-tale hallmark of love and concern; of mutual forgiveness and accommodation; of kindness and tender-heartedness; of interest in the other, of humility.

We should notice that the people who most remind us of Jesus Christ never seem to *say* that they are filled with his Spirit. This was true in the New Testament. It was left to others to observe that Stephen was full of the Holy Spirit; he himself made no such public claim. Of course not – he was always thinking of others and had little time for thinking about himself.

So how do we know if we are filled with the Spirit? We absorb ourselves with the person of Jesus Christ, confessing those things which hinder effectiveness, obeying him in daily life and sharing our energies in selfless love of others. We shall become so involved and fulfilled in the life of the Spirit that we shall forget that we even asked the question.

28 Believing is drinking

*'Why do you spend your money for that which is not bread, and
your labour for that which does not satisfy?'*
  Isaiah 55.2

Is there a chapter like Isaiah 55 anywhere else in the Bible? Written
with the Jewish exiles in Babylonia in mind, it nevertheless
unleashes the universal appeal of God upon every generation of
unsatisfied seekers: 'Ho, every one who thirsts, come to the waters'
(v. 1).

One of the greatest of all English romantic poets, Lord Byron,
once wrote: 'Drank every cup of joy, heard every trump of fame;
drank early, deeply drank; drank draughts which common millions
might have drunk. Then died of thirst, because there was no more
to drink.'

It was a Galilean who sat by a well and said, centuries ahead of
Byron, 'Everyone who drinks of this water will thirst again; but
whoever drinks of the water that I shall give him will never thirst.
The water that I shall give him will become in him a spring of
water welling up to eternal life' (John 4.13). We have to believe, we
may believe, that the divine offer of Isaiah 55 – of satisfaction to
everyone who comes – is an authentic offer, to be accepted by
faith. And what is faith? In the terminology of Isaiah, faith is
coming; faith is buying, without money and without price; faith is
drinking.

An offer of satisfaction

Isaiah's listeners were seen as spending their dwindling resources
on junk foods; but every generation does that. We look for answers
to deeply felt needs in every direction but the right one. At one
point in the 'sixties the Beatles openly admitted, 'We've tried
everything but Christianity.' It was later that John Lennon
declared, 'The dream is over.'

An offer of restoration

The phrases are luminous in their appeal: Seek the Lord while he may be found . . . Let the wicked forsake his way . . . Let him return to the Lord . . . for he will abundantly pardon. God can accomplish in a moment what no man-made philosophy could ever do. The best video technology could never do it. *It is to change the record of our past.* Where else can we find that?

An offer of rejuvenation

The great chapter ends with a picture of the transformation of nature; 'instead of the thorn shall come up the cypress, instead of the brier the myrtle' (v. 13). It is a reversal of the judgement in Genesis 3.17 where Adam was told that the ground was cursed because of him. We come alive again when we have recognized the world of arid unbelief as an empty balloon ride. The way to the new life is the way of coming, of believing, of drinking.

PRAYER

Help me to come alive again, O Lord; awaken me to the world of belief and love and worship. Rejuvenate me and lift me this day, as with eagles' wings. I am coming alive Lord. I am living again. Amen.

29 Snakes and ladders

'Everyone who exalts himself will be humbled, but he who humbles himself will be exalted.'
Luke 18.14

We were all shouting at once as we sat in the kitchen of our London home watching the television. My camera was lined up on the screen – focused on Dennis Taylor poised for a surprise victory in the Embassy World Snooker Championship. My finger began to tighten on the button as Taylor's cue prepared to sink the solitary black ball. Suddenly the screen went fuzzy and we were looking at a snowstorm! 'Do something, someone – quick!' I yelled, camera still pointing at the set. Five seconds of frantic activity followed. Finally the picture cleared. Taylor was still bending motionless over the ball! I got my picture.

The fact is that these moments of drama, when time itself seems to stand still, are so often centred upon the rise of an underdog – or conversely upon the fall of a giant. We love to see the tail-ender forging to the front, the political unknown overturning the election predictions. We may admire the push and the drive that takes a man or woman to the top – but on the whole we do not like pushy people very much. How nice it would be, we think to ourselves, to hear a candid apology from time to time – to hear a political leader say, 'I am sorry, I was wrong.'

But once let the issue come to our own front door, and the difficulty of repenting becomes immediately apparent. On the personal front, nobody likes to be sliding down the snake, when they could be ascending a ladder. The blessedness of humility, of putting others first, of selfless service we all agree with – when it is Mother Teresa of Calcutta who is in view. But there is something in us that recoils from taking the lowest position, that baulks at having to say, 'I am sorry.'

It is a matter of re-education. Ambition itself is neither good nor bad; it is neutral. It is where the drive of ambition is directed that is important. Ambition can create a Hitler – and it can create a Mother Teresa. It is not that we should shun the seeking of greatness. Be great – said Jesus – at serving.

THOUGHT

It was said of one great man whose characteristic was humility:
'It was not that he pretended he was very bad. It was simply that
he had forgotten that he was very good.'

30   Something from nothing

Jesus said to Philip, 'How are we to buy bread, so that these people may eat?' This he said to test him, for he himself knew what he would do.

John 6.5, 6

Why was Philip consulted? Perhaps it was because he was an average-type disciple; he was not particularly gifted, he displayed no dynamic, aggressive characteristics. Jesus selected him for questioning, not as the lowest in the class, but certainly not as the brightest. In a cricket team I might have put him at Number 6, after Peter, James, John, Andrew and Thomas. Here was the group, by the Sea of Galilee, confronted by a vast hungry crowd at the end of an eventful day. Something needed to be done, and Philip was consulted. Why? It was for three reasons.

So that he could be tested

It was not food, but faith, that Jesus wanted from Philip – whose reaction to the question about bread revealed the limitations of his vision. Immediately he began counting on his fingers – fish and chips for five thousand . . . why that's a day's pay, 200 times over. But at least he was made to think about it.

Philip's faith could only rise to the calculating stage – and we must notice that he was only able to calculate what *wouldn't* pay for the food. The whole remarkable event was, for Philip, part of his education in the life of faith.

So that he could be involved

We can imagine the scene near Tiberias, with the crowd growing restless, as Jesus drew Philip on one side for a confidential word. But why ask Philip for advice? The clue is found in John 1.44: 'Now Philip was from Bethsaida.' It was the local man who was going to be involved in the work of Christ. We each have our own neighbourhood, our own circle – and should expect that Philip's privilege will be ours. Your street . . . your crowd . . . how can your local knowledge and role there be used to touch it for God?

So that he could be inspired

Thirdly Philip was deliberately consulted, even though Jesus 'himself knew what he would do'. There was quite a bit to do as well. A young lad allowed his packed lunch to be used. The disciples arranged the crowd in groups easy to handle. Philip had to be consulted. The food was taken out to the crowd; but at the end of the day it was fully conceded that Jesus had done it all. From emptiness had come filling, and it was due to him.

This is part of the encouragement for those caught up in the work of God. We may be at full stretch, and even feel that the demands are beyond us. Good. That will help us to depend even more upon the unseen factor that alone gives our witness its significance and power. We are caught up in the mission of Christ, and are involved as Philip was. But when something is produced from virtually nothing; when results exceed all that we could have hoped for; we shall realize that at every step we were, in reality, watching him at work.

31 Hunger and happiness

'Blessed are those who hunger and thirst for righteousness, for they shall be satisfied.'
  Matthew 5.6

'The church provides the dullest experience going.' So commented a leading showbusiness personality in the pages of *The New Musical Express*. Perhaps we sympathize a little with the statement. It was Dvořák who, on listening once to an Anglican chant, complained, 'Why do they repeat a bad tune so many times?' And was it not Dorothy Sayers who remarked that, while Christ's enemies crucified him, it was left to his disciples to make him dull?

Yet Jesus could never have been described as dull. Not by anybody. What was it that made him special? What was the element in him that captivated the hundreds who swarmed through Galilee to be near him? It was more than mere novelty, and more than an easy offer. He spoke of hard things – of self-denial and taking up the cross. Yet the fascination was still there.

Let's say it. It was his intrinsic, transparent, magnetic *goodness*. Of course the moment we say it, we can feel the let-down. His goodness? Surely it was something more interesting than goodness; something more . . . well, attractive?

It is strange that we equate goodness with dullness. But then we have been conditioned by fiction that does indeed find it hard to make its heroes and heroines appear to be anything more than cardboard cut-outs. It is much easier to present evil! The crime-writers and playwrights know that. It is only when we come to real life itself that we can see goodness in its true riveting attraction. Once we encounter people of real goodness, we never want them to go away. We long to stay in their presence; we feel elevated by their company.

Hence the truth of Christ's words in the Sermon on the Mount, about the blessedness, the happiness, of those who hunger and thirst for righteousness. Their very sense of emptiness will lead to satisfaction. Hungering and thirsting implies real desire. It is more than a casual wish for a touch of morality; it involves a heartfelt longing to be right with God, and to become like Jesus Christ.

It is the hunger and thirst for righteousness that is called 'blessed'

– not the possession of it, even. Indeed, to believe yourself to be in possession of it, like the Pharisee in Jesus' story (Luke 18.11), is absolutely fatal. Then, note again, it is not the thirst for *blessedness*, for happiness, that will bring satisfaction. Once we join the mad search for happiness, we have embarked on a paper-chase after a mirage. Millions are hungering after an *experience*. But when the trip is over and the excitement subsides, we are still in the same bed-sit and nothing has changed; it has all been an illusion.

The Christian is someone who is simultaneously hungering and thirsting, *and being filled*. The marvel of it is that our capacity increases as progress is made. The quest involves a real determination to make time for God, for prayer and the Bible, for fellowship and worship. It involves searching out not necessarily the gifted and the clever, but the godly people; the ones who remind us of Christ, so that we may study with them, pray with them – and go back into our needy world elevated and equipped by our encounter.

When there are enough people in a community who are genuinely concerned, hungering and thirsting after authentic Christ-likeness, no one will ever describe that community as dull.

32 Mary's song

'He has filled the hungry with good things, and the rich he has sent empty away.'
Luke 1.53

It was an Anglican vicar, Eddie Neale, who wrote in his church newspaper column about the communist who attended Evening Prayer at his parish church. The revolutionary concepts of the 'Magnificat' arrested his attention . . . the mighty would be put down . . . the rich would be sent empty away. 'That's marvellous, Vicar!' he exclaimed at the end of the service. 'What shall we do next?'

'Meet at the same time next week,' replied the incumbent, 'and we'll go over the whole thing all over again.'

It is strange how familiarity can blunt even the keenest and sharpest of edges in the world of revolutionary ideas. The stark challenge of Mary's song has tended to become lost in the rhythm of security that the 'Magnificat' has become. But in fact the song represented, in the first place, what Andrew Knowles has called The Messiah's Manifesto – an overturning of the values that governed society of first century Rome and Palestine.

In the new order, as prophetically discerned by Mary, the self-satisfied would be cut down to size dramatically; attainments and endowments amounting to nothing in the divine economy. Emptiness would be their lot. To the poor and empty in spirit – oppressed by a thousand different pressures over the centuries – would be given the 'solid joys and lasting treasure', known only to Zion's children.

The alarming feature about pride is that it can worm its way into virtually every area of our thinking. Of all the manifestations of self-satisfied complacency, the religious is the most hideous of all. It was there among the Pharisees, and it was there among the Corinthian Christians who so despised Paul and rated him as barely an apostle at all: 'For who sees anything different in you? What have you that you did not receive? If then you received it, why do you boast as if it were not a gift? Already you are filled! Already you have become rich! Without us you have become kings!' (1 Cor. 4.7, 8.)

72

These were the most unattractive Christians of all. We might describe them as *the already have's*. They needed nothing; despite their stunted moral stature they strutted about as giants. They could speak the spiritual lingo, but Paul had to describe them as 'carnal', saying that 'your boasting is not good'. We have to read all the Corinthian correspondence with the background knowledge that here was a church with a serious problem.

None of us are inviolate to this deadly sin. 'The real test of being in the presence of God,' wrote C. S. Lewis, 'is that you either forget about yourself altogether or see yourself as a small, dirty object.'

The 'Magnificat' was uttered for our ears.

PRAYER

O Lord God, we pray thee to keep us from all self-confidence and vain glory, and to bestow upon us thy great grace of humility and self-forgetfulness: To thee may we look up, in all that we do, alike for the will and for the power; and to thee may we ascribe with a sincere heart all the praise; through Jesus Christ our Lord. Amen.

Dean Vaughan

GROUP QUESTIONS

The parable of the Pharisee and the tax collector makes a profitable study. After reading Luke 18.9–14, discuss the parable, using the following questions as a springboard for discussion:

1 What was the purpose of Christ's parables? What was the purpose of this parable?
2 Two easily identifiable figures are selected for this story of men at prayer. What would normally have been expected of these two individuals? What would be their modern counterparts?
3 Analyse the prayers and contrast them with each other. With what attitudes were they offered, and what was their main emphasis?
4 What is the purpose of prayer? Why do we bother?
5 Look at verse 14. To be 'justified' biblically means to be accepted by God as righteous. What was it about the tax collector that made it possible for him to be accepted?
6 'I never did anybody any harm' . . . 'I live a decent life' . . . 'I'm not a hypocrite' . . . 'Thank God I'm not like that Pharisee!' What does Christ's parable say to such sentiments?
7 How have Christ's great reversals of human values affected society and the church over the ages? His words about the last being first, and the hungry being filled with good things? What are the areas of weakness that need attention?

PART FIVE

When Poverty is Riches

Wealth is like a viper.

Clement of Alexandria

33   Reversed roles

*'Son, remember that you in your lifetime received your good
things, and Lazarus in like manner evil things; but now he is
comforted here, and you are in anguish.'*
Luke 16.25

The immediate contrast in this story of our Lord's seems to be
between the pauper and the plutocrat. But a closer inspection
shows us that although there is indeed an uncomfortable thrust
here (how quickly we assume that the rich man is someone else, or
some other nation), nevertheless the main issue is one of *choice*.

It is not that Lazarus was accepted into God's security at death
because he is poor, but rather because, in his poverty, he believes.
And the rich man? He was condemned not *because* he was rich, but
because his riches were symptomatic of his godlessness.

This is not exactly a parable. It was never applied by the
narrator; no moral is dragged out of it. It is simply a story, a
sobering story for men and women to hear, and from which to
draw their own conclusions. It is a story of reversal. The plutocrat
is man at his worst, strutting, self-centred godless man. Being an
unbeliever he had nobody to thank. The beggar at his gate he had
never even noticed. Lazarus by contrast is a believer. He has
chosen God. Despite his lamentable circumstances he is richer by
far than his overloaded neighbour; he is destined for the security
of Abraham's bosom. Look carefully now at the over-fed unbeliever. He may be you . . .

His choices were indelible

'Son, remember . . .' Recollections of his past life come flooding
back as the condemned soul sees with hideous clarity how his
choice of the easy way became stamped upon his character; how
what he had been in one life was underlined in the next. As now,
so then! The temptation always is to say to ourselves, 'There's time
still to choose'. Christ's story tells us 'You have already been
choosing for a very long time'.

His defence was unacceptable

'Son remember . . .' Remember that you chose your course during your lifetime? Why grumble now? But the argument of the man, once rich, persists as in torment he begs that his family shall be warned. 'Send Lazarus!' He would still like the poor man to be errand boy on his behalf.

But really there is no excuse – and no need for an emissary to earth. The Jewish nation had been accorded a stream of messengers and prophets; were these not warnings enough? No, comes the protest; let there be a special sign: 'If someone goes to them from the dead, they will repent' (v. 30). The next words were prophetic: 'If they hear not Moses and the prophets, neither will they be persuaded though one rose from the dead' (v. 31).

Who is the rich man of our story? Why, he is Israel. But he also stands for all who have been prospered with opportunity and privilege. In such a case there can be no excuse.

His fate was irreversible

'And besides all this, between us and you a great chasm has been fixed . . .' (v. 26). At a single stroke the picture clears, and both men see their lives as they really were. This final picture is one of permanence and finality. Lazarus has everything; the rich man has nothing. A great reversal has taken place.

'To Fred', a widow once said to me just before the funeral, 'life was one jolly good binge.' It only goes to show that Christ's words were not only for the Jews of his time. They are for every man and woman in every one of our frail civilizations.

34 Empty wealth

*Then I considered all that my hands had done and the toil I had
spent in doing it, and behold, all was vanity and a striving after
wind . . .*

Ecclesiastes 2.11

'Most people,' commented Theophan the recluse, 'are like a
shaving of wood which is curled round its central emptiness.'
Perhaps it is today, as in few other eras, that the book of Ecclesiastes
has truly come into its own as a tract for the times. It brilliantly
exposes the emptiness of life without God – bequeathing us,
through the eyes of Solomon, the third king of Israel, a marvellous
critique of life that has become secularized and devoid of faith in
God. The style of Hebrew in which the book has reached us
indicates that it may have been actually written down somewhat
after Solomon's time, but in all probability Ecclesiastes the
Preacher was Solomon the wise Philosopher and purveyor of
countless proverbs.

In the opening sentences of Ecclesiastes 2, the Preacher sees
wealth in a number of different ways. He sees it in *terms of the
sensual* (vs. 1–3), with his references to pleasure, laughter and
wine. He sees it *in terms of the cultural* (vs. 4–7), as he considers the
building works, vineyards, parks and gardens that have stemmed
from his creative ambition. He conceives of wealth *in terms of the
material* (v. 8) as he recollects the accumulation of silver and gold
that characterized his reign. He thinks of it *in terms of the powerful*
(vs. 9, 10), as he recalls his experience of becoming 'great'.

We sense a change at verse 11: 'Then I considered . . .' What
makes an individual think again about life and its significance?
Very often success itself is the trigger. 'Nothing fails like success,'
said Dean Inge. We scale the summit and are left looking at an
empty sky – what next?

Solomon expressed, centuries ago, the experience that has come
to millions, when we grasp at wealth, and find that we are holding
a shadow. A great many of the fortunes that are being made around
All Souls in London's West End are only paper fortunes. Wealth
by itself can only give an elusive satisfaction, a fleeting security, an
illusory significance.

Used properly, of course money can do wonders. If, however, we imagine that we are a special case and can be trusted to handle money, we had better learn from the humility of John Wesley. In a letter to his sister Patty Hall, he wrote, 'Money never stays with me; it would burn me if it did. I throw it out of my hands as soon as possible, lest it should find a way into my heart . . .' Perhaps it is not surprising, in view of this attitude, that money continued to flow in the direction of Wesley . . . and away again. A Christian industrialist in America put it a little differently: 'As fast as I keep shovelling out,' he said, 'the Lord keeps shovelling in – and the Lord seems to have the bigger shovel.'

It is not money that is the root of all evil. It is the love of it that leads to emptiness, and reduces individuals to little more than a curled-up wood shaving.

PRAYER

Deliver us, Lord, from the love of material things that has destroyed so many. Keep us with a heavenly perspective on such possessions and positions as come our way in this life, that by them we may serve the interests of that better country which is our eternal home.   Amen.

35   A meeting of generous hearts

'I will not offer to the Lord my God sacrifices that have cost me nothing.'
2 Samuel 24.24 GNB

When ideas-men and resource-men get together, the result can be a very pleasing exercise in creativity. So it was in this rather obscure Old Testament episode. A pestilence had ravaged the people of Israel during the reign of David. At its close, the king was urged to build an altar for worship, and the threshing floor of a Jebusite, Araunah by name, was chosen for the site. A meeting was set up for the two men, and it transpired to be a meeting of two generous spirits. Both were prepared to give sacrificially towards a project in which the worship of God was involved. What do they teach us?

Giving is a thing you can do jointly

David put in a bid for the threshing floor, but this was side-stepped by the Jebusite farmer: 'Let my Lord and king take and offer up what seems good to him; here are the oxen for the burnt offering, and the threshing sledges and the yokes of the oxen for the wood. All this, O king, Araunah gives to the king' (2 Sam. 24.22, 23). But David would have none of it. 'No,' he replied, 'but I will buy it of you for a price; I will not offer burnt offerings to the Lord my God which cost me nothing' (v. 24). Eventually a price was agreed and the deal went through.

Joint giving multiplies the potential of a project out of all proportion to the giving strength of the donors. We have proved this in our churches again and again. I tend often to make my calculations to the congregation not in terms of gold bars but Mars Bars. Mention the target figure, and we all shrink visibly. But mention saving the cost of a Mars Bar a day for the next number of months, and the target looks attainable. Provided we do it together.

Giving is a thing you can do strategically

There was thought and care behind David's plan. We find an amplification of the episode in 1 Chronicles 21. It is the same story, except that Araunah's other name 'Ornan' is used. The significant difference, however, lies in the information that David bought not only the threshing floor, but all of the surrounding area – and for what purpose ultimately? It was more than an altar that he had in mind: 'Then David said, "Here shall be the house of the Lord God . . . Solomon my son is young and inexperienced, and the house that is to be built for the Lord must be exceedingly magnificent . . ." ' (1 Chron. 22.1, 5).

So it was through this very simple arrangement, between two generous friends, that the great temple of Solomon took its beginning. Giving at its best has planning and strategy built into it.

Giving is a thing you must do heartily

As we read this little account, we find ourselves attracted by the way in which the two individuals, king and farmer, almost vie with each other in their desire to give generously to the point of sacrifice. True giving stems not so much from a sense of duty as from gratitude for the blessings unleashed upon us by a generous God. A congregation of God's people should not have to be bludgeoned into giving; not if the good news of heaven is being proclaimed and expounded regularly.

Here was a meeting of two generous spirits. They gave sacrificially – to the point of personal cost. But, because the motivation was right, it proved to be an enriching experience.

36   When little is much

'Truly I say to you, this poor widow has put in more than all those who are contributing to the treasury.'

Mark 12.43

Benjamin Franklin, the famous eighteenth-century diplomat and writer, was once listening to the evangelist George Whitefield as he appealed for funds for his orphan project.

Benjamin Franklin resolved, '. . . he should get nothing from me. I had in my pocket a handful of copper money, three or four silver dollar and five pistols in gold. As he proceeded I began to soften, and concluded to give the copper. Another stroke of his oratory determined me to give the silver; and he finished so admirably that I emptied my pockets wholly into the collector's dish, gold and all.'

Motives differ when it comes to Christian giving. Some give on the tip level, sparing a little of their loose change. Some give purely out of habit; instinctively and without thought or planning, their hand fumbles for the customary coin as the collection plate approaches. Some are impulse givers, like Benjamin Franklin – their reponse depends upon the quality of the sermon or the state of their emotions. Just a few give out of ostentation, and it is ironic that Mark's account of the widow with the two coins follows immediately after Christ's exposure of the scribes who, he said, with their long robes and the best seats in the synagogues, would 'devour widows' houses, and for a pretence make long prayers' (Mark 12.38–40). It is the widow who provides us with a model of true giving.

God measures devotion not by our words but by our deeds

For 'measuring' is what he does. There is something deliberate about our Lord's action in sitting opposite the temple treasury and watching the crowds as they pass by the thirteen chests, each inscribed with the intended destination of the offerings. Somehow he was able, sitting there, to discern the offerings that derived from real worship from the actions that only reflected a show-piece religion. The two coins, slipped in by the widow, typified the umpteen jam-jars, missionary boxes and furtively-scrawled-on envelopes, that throughout Christian history have contained the costly offerings of anonymous individuals who gave to the limit.

God measures devotion not by our gifts but by our hearts

It is the motivation that is all-important. It is the planned, thought-out gift that must always be the most satisfying to receive. Christian giving at its best is deliberate, calculating and proportional: 'On the first day of every week, each of you is to put something aside and store it up, as he may prosper . . .' (1 Cor. 16.2).

In the case of the widow, the watchful eye of Christ discerned that she had out-thought and out-given every other donor.

God measures devotion not by what we give but by what we keep

The widow had her limitations. There was no possibility of her giving a silver denarius. She *need* not have given both of her two copper coins, even. One alone would have represented a proportion of fifty per cent. As it was, her entire resources tinkled to the bottom of the temple chest – to contribute to an established religious system that was not without its corruptions, to say the least. That is real giving. Too often our church giving has strings attached; we would like it to be designated towards enterprises over which we have some control. But the temple, with all its deficiencies, represented the very work of God to this widow, and so willingly, unselfconsciously, she gave.

37 Borrowed wealth

The Christian who is poor must be glad when God lifts him up, and the rich Christian must be glad when God brings him down. For the rich will pass away like the flower of a wild plant.
James 1.9, 10 GNB.

'Everything we have is really borrowed,' said Paul Jones, the singer, as he shared his faith, along with his actress wife, Fiona Hendley, on BBC1's *Home on Sunday*. The two of them were telling Cliff Michelmore of the impact that coming to church had first made upon them. Everything had registered – even the collection, as they heard the words from the front: 'All things come from you, O Lord'; and the congregation's response: 'And of your own have we given you.'

The apostle James used poverty and riches to illustrate his theme of the wisdom that we need to cope with life itself, its worries, tangles and frustrations. It is the wisdom that enables a man or woman to cut a straight path through the jungle of temptation, through the hindrances that threaten to obscure the very goal and purpose of life. Where does wealth fit into a successful life?

Irrelevant wealth

The letter of James slams on the head any notion that money is the key to the good life. The man with riches is seen to be no more stable or permanent than the wild poppies in the field; as far as wealth is concerned, it is irrelevant to the central realities of life. If the poor man fails to see this, how frustrated he will always be! If the rich man fails to see it, how empty he will be! Money is a useful tool. To most it is a crushing tyrant.

Transitory wealth

The readers of James' epistle would have understood his terminology about riches fading away like grass. Flowers don't last long in the Middle East. In Port Said, where it rains about once in seven years, the grass flourishes and then fades in a matter of days. It is the same with wealth. We long to buy security with wealth – but security for what? When Paul Getty died he left some 350 million pounds. When the possessor departs, what is the worth of the possession? Life simply has to mean more than this.

Dangerous wealth

Money is only dangerous because it has the power to delude us, to sidetrack us from the adventure and creativity of living upon this planet. But let God colour our thinking, and we begin to make radical adjustments to our treatment of the material and the financial.

When John the Baptist came preaching repentance, his listeners asked him what was involved in repenting. His reply is illuminating. To the crowd he said, 'He who has two coats, let him share with him who has none.' To the tax collectors he said, 'Collect no more than is appointed you.' To the militia he said, 'Rob no one by violence and be content with your wages' (Luke 3.10–14). Three different ways of expressing repentance – *and every single one of them economic*.

PRAYER

Teach us your wisdom, Lord Jesus Christ,
to lay up our treasures
not upon earth, but in heaven;
to set our hearts not on things which pass away,
but on those things which remain for ever.   Amen.

38   The supreme example

For you know the grace of our Lord Jesus Christ, that though he was rich, yet for your sake he became poor, so that by his poverty you might become rich.
  2 Corinthians 8.9

The cross of Golgotha can look to the cynical observer like a dead dry emblem belonging to the dusty archives of history. But not to us. How many of us have sung Thomas Kelly's vivid lines about the unique exchange and transaction effected by the cross:

> The cross he bore is life and health,
>   though shame and death to him;
> his people's hope, his people's wealth,
>   their everlasting theme!

When a man or woman has really seen the cross, life can never be the same again. It becomes the mainspring to all our giving; it galvanizes us into action, it inspires the most amazing feats of self-sacrifice and generosity.

Years ago some of our family were having a picnic on a green hillside just above the harbour of Mombasa on the East African coast. Suddenly one of us tripped on something hard in the undergrowth. It turned out to be a gravestone, completely overgrown. Peering closer, the significance of our discovery became apparent. Ludwig Krapf, the German pioneer missionary, had arrived on the East African coast in 1844, ready to penetrate the interior with the good news of Christ, in fellowship with the Church Missionary Society. Then fever struck. Both his wife and newly-born daughter died and were buried in 'a lonely missionary grave'. Undaunted he carried on with his mission. We spent the rest of the afternoon in clearing up the derelict grave – a solemn reminder of the sheer cost involved in conveying the life-changing message of Christianity to all corners of the earth.

It is still the same. 'Have you noticed', my wife Liz once said to me, 'how so many of our All Souls' representatives overseas seem to end up in the most inhospitable places you could possibly find?' It is all part of a pattern. These ambassadors of Christ's mission have hardly gone for the thrill of travel. Our most recent arrival back from abroad had suffered again and again from ill-health. To cap it all, on coming back for leave, she was beaten up *en route*. Her scars were still showing when she stood up in church one Sunday morning to be greeted by her Christian 'family' who had sent her out.

What is the theology of this? It is the incarnation, and it is Golgotha. The Son of God left the glory of heaven to take manhood upon him and to identify with our sorrows and needs – to the very point of total loss and the indignation of crucifixion. It is as we respond to his love that the incarnation and the cross take a hold upon us. We find ourselves strangely drawn to follow in the steps of Jesus Christ. Our money, our energies, our abilities become placed at his disposal.

It happened to Krapf, and it is happening today. It is going to go on happening, even if you and I opt out of the call to follow the crucified Son of God. He embraced our poverty that we might become rich eternally. Who follows in his train?

REFLECTION

If Jesus Christ be God and died for me, then no sacrifice can be too great for me to make for him.

C. T. Studd
(Cambridge and England cricketer, and missionary pioneer)

39 All things are yours

For all things are yours, whether Paul or Apollos or Cephas or the world or life or death or the present or the future, all are yours; and you are Christ's; and Christ is God's.

1 Corinthians 3.21–23

We have moved a long way since the 'sixties. In that decade the watchword for many was that of 'freedom!' Authority was being defied, old concepts were being overthrown. With the advent of the 'eighties, a new quest made itself apparent. Now the desire was for authority. Strange authoritarian groups began to flourish; people were looking for security – for a cult or personality with whom they could become identified.

This was the picture confronting Paul in the immature church at Corinth. Factions had been set up. In their search for security, men and women were saying, 'I belong to Paul' . . . 'I belong to Apollos' . . . 'I belong to Cephas' – and one precious little group even called themselves the Christ party! (1 Cor. 1.12). It was all very man-centred.

Paul the apostle turned the language of the Corinthians around with a marvellous phrase. 'You say *you belong* to Apollos or Cephas? Do you not realize that *they belong to you*?' In fact 'All things are yours . . .' (1 Corinthians 3.21).

The reasoning is this: Christ has everything; thus the individual who belongs to Christ possesses all things with him – including the very ministers that he had mistakenly thought he himself belonged to. The ministers belong to the church, not the church to the ministers.

Pyramids of authority are out. Divisive factions are out. The true democracy of Christianity centres in an allegiance to Jesus alone. The boasting of the Corinthians resulted in poverty, because it fastened upon the merely human scaffolding of individual personalities. The enriching doctrine of the New Testament is that *All things are yours*.

It is not too difficult to comprehend. Long before I ever saw the centre court at Wimbledon, I felt that in a strange way I owned it. I had read so much about it that when I finally set eyes on it, it was a familiar friend to me. It was 'mine'. It is true of our world. As we

Christians grow in our relationship with Christ, we begin to understand what this world is for, by whom it was originated and where it is heading. Unlike the purveyors of man-made systems, we *do* know something about the reasons for our universe and its existence. Our life in Christ means that it is not a meaningless puzzle any more. It doesn't baffle us, and it certainly is not an enemy. We are beginning to know our way around.

Far more than to the Marxist; far more than to the agnostic who indeed *has* no answers about life and existence; far more than to the existentialist, nihilist or hedonist; *this world belongs to us*. Christ has it all, we are his, he is ours and – as we are told in a final flourish – Christ is God's.

We need that last phrase to tie up the whole argument. It is not to imply the inferiority of the Son. It is, rather, a reminder to us that to belong to Christ is definitely not to belong to yet one more man-made faction or sect; it is to belong to Christ who is in very truth part of the eternal Godhead. Integration and unity are built into this towering concept.

Who owns the world? Why, says Paul, even death is made to serve us, if we belong to Christ . . . all, all is yours.

GROUP QUESTIONS

Study Mark 10.17–22. The passage concerns one of the numerous encounters that Jesus had with individuals. The following questions can serve to promote discussion:

1 Consider the question of Jesus' enquirer, a Jewish leader, as Luke 18.18 informs us. Why did Jesus not give him a direct answer? Why did Jesus so often answer a question with another question?

2 What was the challenge hidden in Christ's return question (v. 18)? What can we learn from our Lord's reply, when we consider our own defence of the Christian faith in the face of questioning?

3 Like so many people, the enquirer imagined that to obtain eternal life there was something that he had to '*do*'. How common is this belief in the group's experience?

4 Christ meets his questioner on his own ground. If indeed eternal life is gained by keeping the law, then what does the law say? But why does Jesus only refer to the commandments that relate to the love of neighbour, and omit those that refer to our love of God?

5 We have no reason to believe that the reply in verse 20 was anything but sincere. Why then was it not acceptable? If Jesus 'loved him' (v. 21) why could he not then and there enlist him?

6 Look at verses 21 and 22. What was it that this rich man 'lacked'? What is the one thing that makes the difference between interest and discipleship?

7 What is it about riches that can hinder us from growing as people and as Christians?

PART SIX

When Losing is Winning

Measure thy life by loss instead of gain
Not by the wine drunk but the wine poured forth
For Love's strength standeth in Love's sacrifice
And he who suffers most has most to give.

Harriet Eleanor Hamilton Smith   *The Disciples*

40 Royalty and humility

Rejoice, rejoice, people of Zion! Shout for joy you people of Jerusalem! Look, your king is coming to you! He comes triumphant and victorious, but humble and riding on a donkey – on a colt, the foal of a donkey.

Zechariah 9.9 GNB

'We're pulling into the side!' Our African driver swung the car away from the centre of the road, and onto the rough verge. Blazing headlights were coming towards us from further up the highway. Sirens were blaring. First a phalanx of motorbike outriders, then armoured cars, travelling like an express train. The tail-end of the motorcade featured a military truck crammed with machine guns and rocket launchers. Somewhere in the middle of the speeding convoy was a Mercedes. In a few seconds the entire cavalcade was a receding speck on the dusty horizon. The President had just gone by . . .

You get used to such sights in certain parts of Africa, where political instability has kept the leadership on edge. It is a pity that it must be so. The world has been longing for a different kind of rule for century upon century:

> Where is your reign of peace
> and purity and love?
> When shall all hatred cease
> as in the realms above?

In the very darkest hours the Jewish nation – buffeted and humiliated by exile, and about to face greater trials yet – was given a vision of hope by Zechariah, the prophet of restoration. The coming king was of the house of David, truly a Messianic figure, and yet combining certain important elements in his person.

A welcome figure

By now the Jews had had their fill of kings. The good ones were conspicuous by their sparseness in the royal line. But here at last was a future king, superior even to David, who would deserve

92

every acclamation that he was accorded. The nation was to be ready with its palm branches. How long it had waited!

A lowly figure

The coming one would be a triumphant ruler, but coming in peace, as suggested by his mount. The image would be instantly recognized on the day that Jesus rode into Jerusalem. No wonder the shouts of joy burst out. But, how was it that so many read into the Old Testament predictions a reign of political revolution?

A weeping figure

Already, on Palm Sunday, the rejection was coming closer. It was as he came closer to Jerusalem that Israel's rightful king began to weep – to weep for the city, to weep for peace, to weep over the opportunities missed by God's people, time without number.

A strange king. He looks a loser rather than a winner. But this was to be the paradox of that Holy Week. The mission of peace, ushered in on the back of a donkey, is a far cry from a speeding convoy of rocket launchers. But it is three thousand times more effective.

PRAYER

Teach us, Lord, to see in your reign of peace and reconciliation the hope of all the nations. Open our eyes, that we may recognize your kingship, beginning with me. For your holy name's sake. Amen.

41   Who wins the kingdom?

'From the days of John the Baptist until now the kingdom of heaven has suffered violence, and men of violence take it by force.'
Matthew 11.12

At the age of sixteen he stood at number 563 in the world tennis ranking lists. One year later at seventeen, he had won the Wimbledon men's singles championships. By the severity of his play and by bold initiative, Boris Becker had ensured a place for himself for all time among the sport's immortals.

It only takes a little determination, a vision of what can be, for a losing position to be changed into a winning one. How often this has been proved. It was never more crucially true than when it began to be apparent that a mighty and divine visitation was taking place in little Galilee. A carpenter-preacher was at work during a period of spiritual transition. It was the beginning of what was called the kingdom of heaven. People were responding to the teaching and mighty works with an enthusiastic fervour, with an excited thronging from the hills and valleys all around. But, why the urgency in 'taking the kingdom by force', as men and women were doing in Galilee, and can be found doing today? It was for three reasons.

Because the difficulties are so many

Those who felt drawn to the Galilean teacher found that there were plenty of obstacles at hand to block their path to him. Take the woman with the haemorrhage who touched the edge of Christ's clothes. Medical history was against her; the law was against her (she was ceremonially unclean), and the crowd was against her. Finally she could only squeeze through the mob and just manage a touch.

Take Bartimaeus the born loser. They wanted to shut him up, but determination kept him shouting ever louder until his needs were met. Take the paralytic at Capernaum. Such was the resolve of his friends to procure the necessary help that they broke up the roof over Jesus' head, in order to lower their patient before him. It is the individual with the holy violence of earnestness and desire who wins the kingdom. But, why the urgency?

94

Because the possibilities are go great

The Roman centurion and his dying servant . . . Jairus and his
ailing daughter . . . Nicodemus and his desire for an interview with
Jesus – all these individuals glimpsed the possibilities that could
result from an encounter with Christ – and they took their chance.
As the tide surged in, during the days of Jesus on earth, so there
were people to be found pressing in upon the kingdom of heaven,
and taking it with all the energy and enthusiasm they could muster.
Again, why the urgency?

Because the opportunities are so fleeting

The kingdom, with its great offer and embrace, sweeps in . . . and
then out again. It is a pattern of life. As we progress in age and
experience, the area of choice available to us tends to shrink and
narrow. Finally when vigour has all but eroded, there are hardly
any more choices open to us; the room for manoeuvre is negligible.

So it is that the door of opportunity is marked *push*. We are
warned once again by the Scribes and Pharisees of old. With
everything on their side – the law, tradition and history – they
nevertheless lost the kingdom. It was the born losers who had
everything against them, who summoned the necessary strength
and vision – and took the kingdom into their lives.

42   When all is lost

*'Our God whom we serve is able to deliver us from the burning
fiery furnace; and he will deliver us . . . But if not, be it known
to you, O king, that we will not serve your gods.'*
Daniel 3.17, 18

That is faith indeed. Here are Shadrach, Meshach and Abednego
facing Nebuchadnezzar's furnace, on account of their stubbornness
in holding onto their convictions. They are convinced that God
will deliver them from their impending fate and they say so. *But if
not* . . .

The fact is that faith in the God of truth brings with it no
guarantee of physical safety. Christians get coronaries just as
unbelievers do. If anybody thinks differently – they have some big
shocks coming their way. The strength, of the three young Hebrews
in Babylon, was that they had the firm conviction they were secure
in the hands of God. Yes, even in the event of their being thrown
into the flames, knowing they might well die. But their security
rested on stronger and firmer factors than the whims of a half crazy
Babylonian despot.

Quite the best thing about the faith of the three Hebrews was its
humility. They did not presume to know God's mind; and they
would not predict the future, being content to let an 'if' remain in
their thinking. They refused to dictate what *must* happen as a result
of their trust. They refused to claim a monopoly as far as guidance
was concerned. Their world did not revolve around their own
narrow circumstances, but around the Creator and his plans.

We tend to run a mile from the bumptious kind of faith that has
everything worked out and neatly pigeon-holed. Perhaps our
greatest source of comfort in the realm of prayers that were not
granted comes from Gethsemane. There our Lord prayed that the
cup of suffering he was about to drink might be taken from him.
Then the 'if' clause was inserted: 'Not my will, but yours be done.'

In the case of the Hebrews, their lives were spared. In the case
of Christ, the cup was drunk willingly, to its very dregs. In both
cases, the will of God was fulfilled. And his will is perfect.

Father, although I cannot see
    the future you have planned,
and though the path is sometimes dark
    and hard to understand:
yet give me faith, through joy and pain,
    to trace your loving hand.

When I recall that in the past
    your promises have stood
through each perplexing circumstance
    and every changing mood,
I rest content that all things work
    together for my good

Whatever, then, the future brings
    of good or seeming ill,
I ask for strength to follow you
    and grace to trust you still;
and I would look for no reward,
    except to do your will.

John Eddison

43 A tale of two cities

'And Jerusalem shall be holy and strangers shall never again pass through it' . . . *'For the days shall come upon you, when your enemies will cast up a bank about you and surround you . . .'*
Joel 3.17; Luke 19.43

Jerusalem . . . perhaps the oldest city in the world, and certainly one of the oldest. But of which Jerusalem are we thinking? Is it the city of Joel chapter 3 – the city of God, the city of plenty and the city of peace?

History depicts Jerusalem as a city of destruction. It was conquered by Joshua and more particularly by David. Nebuchadnezzar destroyed the city and the temple in the sixth century BC. Later, the Jews were able to rebuild the shattered walls, but the fourth century saw the city taken by Ptolemy. In 170 BC the infamous king, Antiochus Epiphanes, took Jerusalem, desecrating the temple and dedicating a new altar there to Zeus, of whom he himself claimed to be an incarnation. Through the valiant efforts of Judas Maccabeus, the Jews rallied and re-dedicated the temple – and Jerusalem was free once more.

In 63 BC the Roman general Pompey marched into Jerusalem; a Parthian army plundered it in 40 BC; Herod the Great re-took the city and began to build the temple once more. But then in 70 AD, with the revolt of the Jews against Rome, Jerusalem fell after a siege, and the temple was once again smashed to pieces. In 132 AD the emperor Hadrian rebuilt Jerusalem as a pagan city. This changed in the fourth century with Constantine. But in 614 the city was stormed by the Persians, recovered by the Byzantines, only to be taken by the Muslims in 637. In 1099 Jerusalem was captured by the Crusaders, then re-conquered by Saladin in 1187. The Ottoman Turks took it in 1517; in 1542 Suleiman the Magnificent rebuilt its walls. Then in 1917 General Allenby marched in. In 1948 the city was divided between Arabs and Jews. Only a few years ago, the Israelis took the city with the determination never to let it go.

It is an amazing saga of physical destruction, of layer upon layer of rubble. And yet, there is the idealistic side that we are given in the Bible, with its references to a stream of water flowing from the temple (Ezekiel 47) – language that is paralleled in Zechariah 14.8, and by Jesus in John chapter 4. Revelation 22 speaks to us of the city of God, the new Jerusalem, with its perfect proportions, its sure security and its flowing river. Perfect harmony and fellowship will exist there; all impurity will be excluded.

The two cities bear no comparison, one with another – and yet there is a relationship. The eternal City of God, which is our true home, is related to the far from perfect Jerusalem, that has been flattened and flattened over the centuries. Jesus wept over this city which so soon was to suffer total loss. But it was by his death that the new Jerusalem would come into being, one day to be united to him as a bride adorned for her husband. There will be no more death, no more destruction, no more grief or pain. The old things will have disappeared.

We, who by virtue of our relationship to Christ are called the New Jerusalem, owe it all to the one who makes all things new.

44   A new era

'I have earnestly desired to eat this passover with you before I suffer; for I tell you I shall not eat it until it is fulfilled in the kingdom of God.'
  Luke 22.15, 16

It was Passover time in Jerusalem, the night before Jesus went to his death. The end was very near. One of his own friends had already sold him for money to their enemies. Jesus was wishing the moment nearer when he could join with his friends in the Passover meal.

Anticipation

In this fellowship meal, Christ would find strength and support for the ordeal that lay ahead. The divine and the human are interwoven here. Before Jesus there awaited a soul-searing experience; it was no play-acting that made him recoil. But there was another reason for his eagerness to sit at the table with his companions.

Transition

He called the gathering the 'passover', and yet he was transforming it. This was the night when the salvation and deliverance from Egypt centuries earlier was celebrated. The cup of wine was blessed, the bitter herbs were eaten, the second cup was passed round the company and the meaning of the Passover was explained. The two unleavened loaves were consumed, together with part of the sacrificial lamb and the herbs; the feast concluding with the distributon of a third and then a fourth cup. During the evening the meal was being changed into the new ordinance of the Lord's Supper. This was the night of transition.

Institution

Here then was a new service: 'This is my body' . . . 'This is my blood' . . . 'Take and eat' . . . 'Drink this'. Christ left us no memorial stone, no tablets. He never even wrote a book. He simply commanded his followers to remember him in a family meal. We have been doing it ever since.

His body broken once for us
  is glorious now above;
the cup of blessing we receive,
  a sharing of his love:
as in his presence we partake,
  his dying we proclaim
until the hour of majesty
  when Jesus comes again.

Christopher Porteous

45 Turning point

'This is your hour, and the power of darkness.'
Luke 22.53

There are a number of breakthrough points in the world's history, when life could never be quite the same again. The discovery of America, the invention of the internal combustion engine, the advent of great intellects: Galileo, Newton, Einstein. But all these must pale before the great event which Jesus Christ referred to so often as 'my hour'.

When he was finally seized, however, Jesus described it as 'your hour' to his enemies. All of history comes down to this one point and event. It is full of mystery and paradox.

The hour where accident and design converged

The cross can be interpreted from one viewpoint as the tragic martyrdom of an upright man. His foes were set on his death; one of his band sold him for money, and after a travesty of a trial he was handed over to be crucified.

Yet this is only the smaller part of it. Christ repeatedly warned his friends of what was going to take place. The Son of Man had come 'to give his life as a ransom for many' (Mark 10.45). He is the Lamb slain from the foundation of the world. The design of redeeming love was behind the death of Christ.

The hour where evil and good clashed

'Your hour', Christ called it to his arresters. Earlier he had called it 'my hour'. Here is the high watermark of sin – but it is also the apex in the revelation of the goodness of God. It was the hour of treachery, but it was the hour of salvation too.

The hour where defeat and victory coincided

He called it 'your hour' – and it is with relief that we recognize it to have been only an hour. This was the summit of evil, but it was also evil's limit. It was no pantomime; the pain was real and the blood was human. It was a terrible death and the whole of the Jesus event looked to have ended in utter, abject failure. Our Muslim friends cannot bear to think that Jesus actually died upon a cross; the theory of Islam is that a substitute was found to take Christ's place.

But it happened before many witnesses in the public gaze outside Jerusalem. It looked like defeat as the darkness closed in upon Jesus' final agony. And yet, as he cried out, 'It is finished!' Jesus signalled that his purpose in coming to earth was achieved. Sin had been atoned for; evil had been overcome; death had been vanquished. It was victory.

MEDITATION

The real clue had been put into my hand by that hard-boiled atheist when he said, 'Rum thing, all that about the dying God. Seems to have really happened once.'

C. S. Lewis in *Surprised by Joy*

46 Changing sides

'Jesus, remember me when you come into your kingdom.'
   Luke 23.42

I once showed a dying man the Bible's best known sentence, from a small pocket Gospel. I read the words out slowly: 'For God so loved the world that he gave his only begotten Son, that whosoever believeth in him should not perish but have everlasting life' (John 3.16 AV).

'You can put your own name there if you like,' I said. 'God so loved Ken . . .' and on I went explaining it. Finally, the patient in the hospital bed reached out for the little Gospel and, with a ballpoint pen, put a bracket round the famous John 3.16 verse. Then he carefully placed a tick in the margin. He had had very little Christian background, but his meaning was unmistakable. He believed. He asked to be baptized the next day, and a few hours later he had slipped away from this life.

Perhaps such death-bed repentances are limited in number, but they happen. Augustine said, 'There is one case of death-bed repentance recorded, in order that no one should despair, but only one, in order that no one should presume.'

The penitent thief has riveted the attention of many throughout history. What a difficult moment in which to pray! The immobility of pain-wracked arms and feet, the torturing thirst, the exposure to public view . . . But there was something about his companion on the next cross, something that awoke him to the reality of the kingdom of Christ. It may have been the very silence of Jesus in the face of the mocking jeers of his enemies and of the other thief. It may also have been the voice of Christ – when the central figure spoke at all, it was with words of love and forgiveness.

One bound of faith and he was there. We, who find it hard or inconvenient to believe, let us learn from the thief. Somehow he became aware that his fellow-sufferer was destined for a place of security and peace.

'Remember me,' he murmured. 'Take me with you.' This is the amazing power of Jesus Christ. Even when on the cross in his greatest extremity, he had the power to take others with him to the tranquillity of paradise. But, of course, it was through his suffering that the gateway to heaven was opened at all.

There is hope for us all. It was Richard Baxter, the famous seventeenth century Puritan leader and hymn writer, who once commented with enthusiasm on the 'Whosoever' of John 3.16: 'I thank God for this word "Whosoever",' he declared. 'Did it read, "There is mercy for Richard Baxter, *I* am so vile, so sinful, that I would have thought it must have meant some other Richard Baxter; but this word "Whosoever" includes the worst of all the Baxters that ever lived!'

GROUP QUESTIONS

Ephesians 2.1–10 makes a good study. When you have considered the passage in the group, discussion can be based upon the questions below:

1 The apostle Paul is writing to young Christians at Ephesus. How does he describe their condition before they were believers in Christ? (vs. 1–3).

2 How far would you use these descriptions of the unbelieving world around us today?

3 Look at verse 4 onwards. Trace the verbs used of God's action in regard to members of his church. What has he done for us? How would we put this into modern words?

4 From this passage, how could we help a friend who assumed that we could earn God's favour by doing good deeds? How would we put this into our own words?

5 What is the place of 'works' or good deeds in the life of a Christian? At what point do we discount them? When do they come into their own?

6 Pick out the instances in this passage where the terms 'with Christ' or 'in Christ' occur. What are these phrases telling us about Jesus Christ?

7 Can members of the group pick a phrase from the passage which they would like to turn into a prayer, either spoken or silent?

EPILOGUE

47 The last laugh

'Why do you seek the living among the dead?'
Luke 24.5

I have heard it said that some American hospitals do not use the term 'death' in their wards. They prefer the term 'negative patient output'. On the whole we could cope better with death two or three hundred years ago; it was close to us most of the time. Today, our health services have pushed the subject further and further away and we try not to face it. It comes, nevertheless, to quote Stephen Travis, as 'the hardest fact of all. It comes like the tide which destroys the sandcastle and makes it as though it had never existed' (*I Believe in the Second Coming*).

Certainly death seemed to have wiped out every vestige of hope among the scattered disciples on that dreadful day of their master's fate. Everything had come to an agonizing, grinding halt. The world's supposed Messiah had been killed like a criminal. Evil had conquered; the sun's light had failed and darkness had taken over. Chaos now ruled and everything was reduced to a meaningless jigsaw puzzle.

But no, the Galilean it was who had the last, the ultimate, laugh. 'What are you doing here among the tombs?' asked the angelic messengers of the women on Sunday morning. It was hardly the right place to begin a search for the Lord of Life. Before long there were running footsteps everywhere as the excitement mounted. Christ really was alive, not just as a beautiful idea or a memory, but literally and historically, bodily and visibly. It was this, and nothing else, that so transformed the disciples and turned them into an indomitable band of evangelists. The worst that could possibly have happened had taken place, and on that wonderful Easter Sunday, the tables had been turned dramatically.

Easter makes us all think again. It means that we have to revise our thinking about death, about Christ, and about the future. A man has gone to the grave and come back again to be its everlasting conqueror on behalf of all mankind. It is he, who by his living presence, is able to lift whole civilizations; to banish the spectre of Old Man Death – and to set the footsteps running . . . everywhere.

Christ triumphant, ever reigning,
Saviour, Master King!
Lord of heaven, our lives sustaining,
hear us as we sing:
Yours the glory and the crown,
the high renown, the eternal name.

Michael Saward

ACKNOWLEDGEMENTS

Unless otherwise stated, all biblical quotations are from the *Revised Standard Version* of the Bible, copyrighted 1946, 1952, © 1971, 1973 by the Division of Christian Education of the National Council of the Churches of Christ in the USA, and are used by permission. All rights reserved.

Biblical quotations from the Holy Bible, *New International Version.* Copyright © 1973, 1978, International Bible Society. Published by Hodder and Stoughton.

Biblical quotations from the *Good News Bible*, © American Bible Society 1976, published by the Bible Societies/Collins, are used by permission.

Page 4 'like your landlord' is taken from *Rhinoceros* by Simon Jenkins, © Fool Press 1980, used by permission.

Page 41 The verse from 'Freedom and life are ours', copyright © Christopher Idle (from *Hymns for Today's Church*) is used by permission.

Page 97 The hymn 'Father although I cannot see' by John Eddison, copyright © Scripture Union, is used by permission.

Page 101 'His body broken once for us . . .' taken from 'He gave his life in selfless love', copyright © Christopher Porteous (from *Hymns for Today's Church*) is used by permission.

Page 109 The verse from 'Christ triumphant, ever reigning', copyright © Michael Saward (from *Hymns for Today's Church*) is used by permission.